Ex
Libris

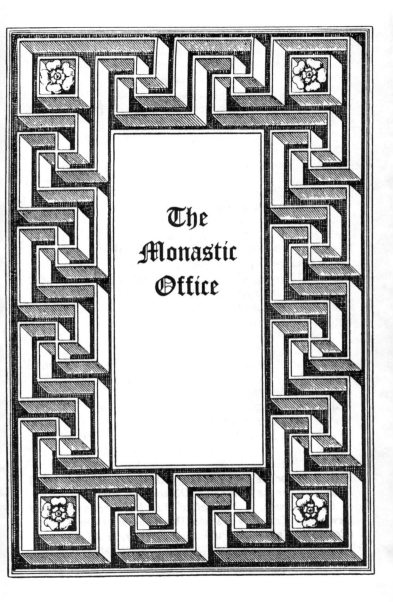

The
Monastic
Office

Translated from the *Sōtō-Shu Gyōji Kihan*
(The Ceremonial Practices of the Sōtō Church)
by Rev. Hubert Nearman, O.B.C.
(Dr. Mark J Nearman).

Consultant and editor,
Rev. Master P.T.N.H. Jiyu-Kennett, M.O.B.C.

First Edition—July 1993.
First Printing—July 1993.
© 1993 Rev. Master P.T.N.H. Jiyu-Kennett, M.O.B.C.
All rights reserved.
Shasta Abbey Press, P.O. Box 199,
Mt. Shasta, California 96067;
(916) 926-4208.

For the newly published ceremonies in *The Monastic Office,*
Rev. Hubert Nearman, O.B.C., used the 1974 edition (the
supplementary revised edition for the Shōwa Era) of the *Sōtō-shū Gyōji Kihan*, edited by the Religious Studies Section
(Tokyo: Sectarian Affairs Department, Sōtō Church, 1974).
The newly published Scriptures in *The Monastic Office* are
translations of texts from the *Taishō Daizōkyō* made by Rev.
Nearman with Rev. Master P.T.N.H. Jiyu-Kennett, M.O.B.C.,
as consultant and editor. Material previously published by
Rev. Master Jiyu-Kennett included in *The Monastic Office*
originally appeared in *Selling Water by the River* (1972), *Zen
is Eternal Life* (1976 and 1987), *The Liturgy of the Order of
Buddhist Contemplatives* (1987), *The Liturgy of the Order of
Buddhist Contemplatives for the Laity* (1987 and 1989), *The
Shasta Abbey Book of Ceremonies* (1979) and/or *The Shasta
Abbey Psalter* (1979). The music for the *Adoration of the
Buddha's Relics* is the Russian *Kontakion of the Departed.*

Printed in the United States of America.
ISBN 0-930066-14-6

This book is dedicated to
all true disciples of the Buddha.

CALENDAR.

page

Every Day

Pre-Dawn Office Avalokiteshwara
(Kanzeon) Ceremony 1.
Morning Office 10.
Morning Service 31.
Founder's Ceremony 38.
Scriptural Recitation for the Lord of
the Kitchen Stove 52.
Dining Hall Ceremonial and Abridged
Procedure for Food Altar 53.
Shurangama Ceremony 56.
Mid-Day Service 76.
Evening Office 82.

First Day

Scriptural Recitation for Sending Bless-
ings to the President and Prayers
for the Peace of the Nation 87.
Scriptural Recitation for the Guardian
Deity 90.
Commemorative Service for the
Arahants 92.
Offering to Shakyamuni Buddha 95.
The Reading Aloud of *Rules of the
Trainees' Hall* 97.

Third Day

    Mindful Recitation for the Closing of
        the Meditation Hall   104.

Fourth Day

    Opening the Baths   107.
    Memorial for the Death of Great
        Master Bodhidharma   111.

Fifth Day

    Scriptural Recitation for Skanda   113.
    Monthly Celebration for Great Master
        Bodhidharma   116.

Eighth Day

    Mindful Recitation for the Closing of
        the Meditation Hall   104.

Ninth Day

    Opening the Baths   107.
    Memorial for the Death of Great
        Master Bodhidharma   111.

Eleventh Day

    The Reading Aloud of *Rules of the
        Trainees' Hall*   97.

Thirteenth Day

Mindful Recitation for the Closing of
the Meditation Hall   104.

Fourteenth Day

Opening the Baths   107.
Memorial for the Death of Great
Master Bodhidharma   111.
Abridged Form of Renewal of Vows   117.
Evening Spiritual Examination and
Serving of Tea   126.

Fifteenth Day

Scriptural Recitation for Sending Bless-
ings to the President and Prayers
for the Peace of the Nation   87.
Scriptural Recitation for the Guardian
Deity   90.
Commemorative Service for the
Arahants   92.
Offering to Shakyamuni Buddha   95.

Eighteenth Day

Mindful Recitation for the Closing of
the Meditation Hall   104.

Nineteenth Day

Opening the Baths   107.
Memorial for the Death of Great
    Master Bodhidharma   111.

Twenty First Day

The Reading Aloud of *Rules of the
Trainees' Hall*   97.

Twenty Third Day

Mindful Recitation for the Closing of
    the Meditation Hall   104.

Twenty Fourth Day

Opening the Baths   107.
Memorial for the Death of Great
    Master Bodhidharma   111.

Twenty Eighth Day

Mindful Recitation for the Closing of
    the Meditation Hall   104.
Memorial Service for the Deaths of
    the Two Ancestors Dōgen and
    Keizan   128.

Twenty Ninth Day

Opening the Baths   107.

Memorial for the Death of Great
    Master Bodhidharma   111.

Monthly Celebration for the Two
    Ancestors Dōgen and Keizan   131.

Thirty First Day

· Abridged Form of Renewal of Vows   117.

Evening Spiritual Examination and
    Serving of Tea   126.

SPECIAL MONTHLY CEREMONIES.

page

__Every Month__

      Monthly Celebration for the Founder
         of One's Temple   137.
      Monthly Celebration for a Venerable
         Elder or Previous Abbot   139.

__First Month__

26th Day: The Festival of the Birth of the
           Highest Ancestor Dōgen   140.

__Second Month__

1st Day: Reading of *The Scripture of the
           Buddha's Last Teachings*   151.

9th Day: Mindful Recitation at the Shrine of
           the Guardian Deity   167.
           Reading of *The Scripture of the
           Buddha's Last Teachings*   171.

16th Day: The Opening of the Guest House   172.

__Fourth Month__

1st Day: The Shutting Down of the Furnaces   173.

Fifth Month

1st Day: The Closing of the Guest House   174.

14th Day: Mindful Recitation at the Shrine of
the Guardian Deity   175.
The Offering of Tea by the Senior
Officers of the Temple   176.

15th Day: Circumambulation of the Dormitories   181.
Abridged Form of Renewal of Vows   117.

16th Day: Commemorative Service for the
Arahants   92.
Head Novice's Presentation of a
Fundamental Doctrine and Tea   184.

Sixth Month

13th Day: Great Festival of the Renewal of
Vows   187.

Seventh Month

2nd Day: Opening of Baths for Summer   188.

30th Day: Great Festival of the Renewal of
Vows   187.

Eighth Month

14th Day: Mindful Recitation at the Shrine of
the Guardian Deity   189.

16th Day: The Opening of the Guest House   172.

Ninth Month

29th Day: Memorial for the Two Ancestors
           Dōgen and Keizan   190.

Tenth Month

5th Day: Memorial for Great Master
           Bodhidharma   111.

Eleventh Month

1st Day: The Closing of the Guest House   174.
           The Turning on of the Furnaces   191.

14th Day: Mindful Recitation at the Shrine of
             the Guardian Deity   192.
           The Offering of Tea by the Senior
             Officers of the Temple   193.

15th Day: Circumambulation of the Dormitories   181.

16th Day: Commemorative Service for the
             Arahants   92.
           Head Novice's Presentation of a
             Fundamental Doctrine and Tea   184.

21st Day: Festival of the Birth of the Greatest
             Ancestor Keizan   194.

Twelfth Month

10th Day: Memorial for the Second Chinese
             Ancestor Taisō Eka   195.

13th Day: Sweeping Out the Soot from Various
            Halls   196.

31st Day: Mindful Recitation at the Shrine of
            the Guardian Deity   197.

SCRIPTURES.

Adoration of the Buddha's Relics	43.
Ancestral Line	24.
The Golden Bell that Rings but Once	85.
Invocation for the Removal of Disasters	114.
Invocation of Achalanatha	84.
Invocation of Mahakala	85.
Invocation of the Cosmic Buddha	85.
The Litany of the Great Compassionate One	39.
The Most Excellent Mirror—Samādhi	18.
The Names of the Ten Buddhas	104.
Rules for Meditation	77.
Rules of the Trainees' Hall	98.
Sandōkai	16.
The Scripture of Avalokiteshwara Bodhisattva	2.
The Scripture of Great Wisdom	33.
The Scripture of the Buddha's Last Teachings	152.
The Scripture on the Conduct that Eases the Way	140.
The Scripture on the Immeasurable Life of the Tathagata	131.
The Shurangama Litany	56.

PRE-DAWN OFFICE
AVALOKITESHWARA (KANZEON)
CEREMONY.

Special note: This ceremony takes place directly after the end of the Achalanatha ceremony and ends just before the wake-up bell is rung.

Acolytes, chaplain or celebrant: Light candle and powdered incense box on the Avalokiteshwara altar and prepare one lighted stick of incense: the heavenly canopy may be lit if so desired.

Celebrant and chaplain (if present): Process from abbot's vestry or private room to Avalokiteshwara altar: celebrant wears white robe, formal robe, Kesa and carries mat and lotus sceptre: chaplain carries lighted stick of incense.

Chaplain: Stand in the usual chaplain's place in the Avalokiteshwara Chapel and behave throughout as a chaplain would for a memorial ceremony.

Celebrant: Walk to the altar in the usual way: there offer incense, stick and powdered, in the usual way, asking for the help of Avalokiteshwara for oneself and the community throughout the next twenty-four hours: return to the bowing seat in the normal way, spread full mat and make three bows in the usual way whilst reciting one of the *Three Homages* silently with each bow.

Chaplain: If present, make three bows together with the celebrant with folded mat: ring the signal gong for the three bows.

Celebrant

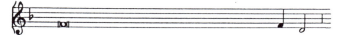

The Scripture of Avalokiteshwara Bodhi - satt - va *

Organ

Tonus Peregrinus.

Celebrant and chaplain

In | verse, Mujinni Bodhisattva | asked, :
  "World | Honoured One, po|ssessor of all grace, ||
What | reason is there for the Buddha's | Son, :
Great | Kanzeon, to | thus be so addressed?" ||
The | Honoured One made answer too in | verse, :
"Just | listen to the | life of Kanzeon. ||
To | calls from every quarter He re|sponds; :
Of | oceanic | depth His holy vows. ||

* A | myriad Buddhas has He truly | served :
For | ages past be|yond the thought of man ||
† And | made for aye great | vows of purity. ||
When | people hear His name, and see His | form, :
And | think of Him not | vainly in their hearts, ||
† All | forms of ill, in | all the worlds, shall cease. ||
If, | wishing harm, an enemy should try to push another
   in a fiery | pit, :
The | victim should, on Kanzeon's great power, think, —
   and straightway that fiery pit shall be transformed
   into a | cool and silver lake. ||
If, | drifting in the vast great ocean's foam, — a man
   should be in danger of his life from monstrous fish
   or evil | beings, :
Let | him only think on Kanzeon's great power, — at
   once the sea will | all compassion be. ||
If, | from the top of Sumeru, — a man be hurled down
   by an enemy's cruel | hand, :
Just | let him think on Kanzeon's great power and, —
   like the sun, he | will remain aloft. ||
If, | chased by wicked men, — a man should fall upon
   a | mountain, :
Let | him think again of Kanzeon's power — and no
   injury will e'en a single | hair of him sustain. ||
If, | ringed by enemies, — a man should be threatened
   by them, — all with their swords in | hand, :

Just | let him think on Kanzeon's great power, —
    compassion then with | in their hearts will dwell. ||
When | tyrants persecute a man — and he stands at the
    place of exe | cution :
Let | him only think on Kanzeon's great power, — the
    executioner's | sword will broken be. ||
If, | bound in chains, — in prison, — let a man just
    think on Kanzeon's great holy | power, :
At | once the shackles | will then set him free. ||
When | poisonous herbs, — or magic, threaten | harm, :
The | power of Kanzeon, — if thought upon, — will
    quickly send the | curse back whence it came. ||
If | poisonous creatures, — evil ones, should | come, :
U | pon great Kanzeon's power gently dwell, — straight-
    way those evil | ones dispersed will be. ||
When | snakes and scorpions attack a man, — exhaling
    evil poisons, | scorching him, :
By | dwelling on great Kanzeon's holy power — they
    will be turned a | way with shrieks of fear. ||
When | lightning flashes and the thunder rolls, — when
    hailstones beat and rain in torrents | pours, :
The | power of Kanzeon, — if thought upon, — will
    quickly clear the | heavens of the storm. ||
If, | struck by cruel disaster's evil hand — or tortured
    by interminable pain, — a being flees to Kanzeon's
    gentle | arms :

He, | being wise and full of mystic power, — will save
him from all | worldly grief and care. ||

With | all miraculous powers well en|dowed :
And | widely skilled in | knowledge of all things, ||
In | all the world, in all the | quarters, :
There | is not a place where | Kanzeon does not go. ||

Hells, | evil spirits, — beastly creatures, — all the evil
ways of living, — all the pain that comes from
birth, old age, disease and | death :
Will, | for eterni|ty, all pass away. ||

Great | Kanzeon views all the world in | Truth, :
Free | from defilement, | loving, knowing all, ||
Full | of com|passion; :
He | must always be prayed to, — adored for | all
eternity. ||

He | is a Light pure, — spotless, like the | sun, :
With | wisdom does He darkness all dispel, subverting
all e|ffects of wind and fire; ||
† His | all-illuming | light fills all the world. ||

As | thunder shakes the universe does He control His
loving | body :
And | His thought of great compassion, — like a cloud
from which a rain of Dharma comes, as nectar,
down, — destroys the flames of | evil passions all. ||

When, | threatened by court judgments or, in camp, —
the military should a man op|press, :

Let | him but think on Kanzeon's great power — and all
his | enemies will be dispersed. ||

* He | is a most exquisite Voice, — a Voice that all the
world encompas|ses; :

The | Voice of Brahma, — Voice of oceans — One
that all the voices of the | world does much excel, ||

† Be|cause of this our thought must | always dwell upon
Him. ||

Let | us never cherish thoughts of doubt about great
Kanze|on :

Who | is all pure and holy and a refuge true, — *
protecting in all grief, — in | trouble, death,
disaster. ||

He | possesses merit all, — regards all things with a
compassionate eye and, — like the ocean, — holds
within Himself a mass of virtues inestima|ble, :

† For | this He must for | ever be adored." ||

Then | rose up from his seat Jiji Bo|satsu :

To | stand before the | Buddha, saying thus, ||

"World | Honoured One, — they, who this Scripture
hear of Kanzeon Bo|satsu, :

Must | indeed no small a|mount of merit gain ||

For | here His life of perfect | action is described. ||

This | is the life of One Who, — all endowed with
powers all mir|aculous, :

Ap|pears in | all directions." ||

When | the Buddha thus finished the recitation in
the | hall :
Of | this great Scripture which makes clearly plain —
the life and work of | the All-Sided One, ||
All | people present then, — a great concourse, — in
number four and eighty thousand | strong, :
+ With | all their hearts | cherished a longing deep ||
+ For | the Supreme Enlightenment with | which :
No|thing in all the | universe compares. ||

Chaplain: Intone or recite the following
offertory

Whole - heartedly do we recite this Scripture.

We offer the merits thereof, candles, flowers,

and fruit to Kanzeon,

the Great Compassionate Bodhisattva, Who

is . . our ex - am - ple.

When - ever this Scripture is recited Great

Compassion is with us

and we are searching for It with-in our - selves.

We pray for peace in all the world;

we pray that evil may be overcome by good;

we pray for the peace of this church and

for the cessation of all . . dis - ast - er . . . . . .

Organ, celebrant and chaplain

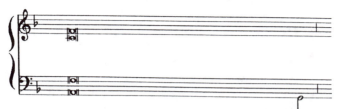

* Homage   to   all   the   Buddhas   in   all   worlds,

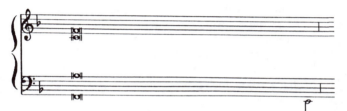

* Homage   to   all   the Bodhisattvas in   all   worlds,

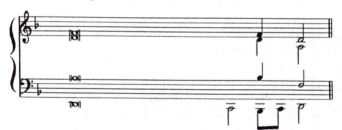

* Homage   to   the Scripture of Great   Wis – dom.

Celebrant and chaplain: Make three bows in the usual way whilst silently reciting one of the *Three Homages* with each bow: pick up and fold mats: make three gratitude bows in the usual way.

MORNING OFFICE.

Head novice's assistant: Thirty minutes prior to the commencement of morning meditation strike the time block for the purpose of awakening the head novice.

Head novice: Ring the awakening bell fifteen minutes prior to the commencement of meditation.

Community: During the quarter of an hour that elapses from the time of the awakening bell until the time block which is struck to announce the entry of the abbot, or master, in charge of the meditation for that day, trainees may use the toilet, wash their hands, wash out their mouths and wash their faces: no words must be uttered during the toilet and washing procedures: washing, dressing and the stowing of bedding in the cupboards provided in the meditation hall must be completed prior to the striking of the abbot's, or master's, time block: once the time block is struck no novices, except the head novice and his assistant, may enter the hall: in addition to the above, the time block is struck to warn those who have not yet settled down on their seats to do so quickly since the appearance of the master of the day is imminent.

Head novice's assistant: Strike the time block at the time appointed for the commencement of meditation.

Head novice: When the time block is struck, offer the morning incense in the following manner: holding the morning incense stick, already alight, stand just inside the door, and to the left, beside the instruments in bad weather and outside the door, on the left side, facing away from the hall, in good weather: at the sound of the time block, enter the hall at the left side of the door with the left foot: cross the hall at the bottom of the bowing seat: go up the right side of the bowing seat: take three side-steps to the left in front of the incense altar, make monjin and offer the incense stick: make monjin with hands in gasshō, then take three side-steps to the right: turn anticlockwise to come down what is now your left side of the bowing seat: spread the mat, folded, at a place at the bottom of the bowing seat and make three full bows: take up the mat and turn aside to fold it: go to the table for the Sword of Buddha's Wisdom: hold up the Sword of Buddha's Wisdom at the bottom of the bowing seat and make monjin: go up your left side of the bowing seat, behind the altar and back down the other side of the bowing seat: turn the Sword of Buddha's Wisdom, blade downwards and go around the hall, first making monjin to the abbot's seat, starting at the seat of the head novice's zealator/zealatrix and finishing at your own: at each of the Four King seats, side-step and make monjin: step out of the hall, on the abbot's side of the door, using the left foot: go around the gaitan in a similar manner to that in which you went around the hall: return to the left side of the door and again enter with the left foot: place the Sword of Buddha's Wisdom upon its table and return to your own seat via the back of the altar.

Celebrant: Wearing white robe, formal robe, Kesa and carrying mat and Sword of Buddha's Wisdom, enter the meditation hall as the head novice commences his round at the seat of the abbot's chaplain: celebrant brings his own Sword of Buddha's Wisdom since head novice is using the meditation hall one.

Precentor: Ring the small bell three times as the celebrant enters the hall: the ringing of the bell should therefore synchronize both with the celebrant's entry and with the commencement of the head novice's round of the hall.

Special note: If the celebrant is not the abbot, the following is done: if the celebrant is the abbot, the procedure is somewhat different.

Acolyte: Have a lighted stick of incense ready to hand to the chaplain.

Chaplain: Receive the stick of incense from the acolyte in the usual way.

Celebrant: Mount the bowing seat and make monjin: spread the mat fully and make three bows: go to the altar, receive the incense stick from the chaplain and offer it in the usual way: do not offer powdered incense: return to the bowing seat in the usual way and make monjin.

Chaplain: Assist with the incense offering in the usual way, then go to your seat and sit down after celebrant starts around the hall.

Celebrant: Holding the Sword of Buddha's Wisdom horizontally, leave the bowing seat and go round the altar to make monjin to the abbot: then go around the meditation hall in the opposite direction to that taken by the head novice, starting and ending at prior's tan, and including gaitan: monks make gasshō while he bows at their tans: on returning to the foot of the bowing seat, at the end of the round, walk onto the bowing seat, hold the Sword of Buddha's Wisdom and make monjin: leave the bowing seat by the back and go to your seat, using the usual route taken in the meditation hall, and sit down.

Precentor: As soon as the celebrant is seated, ring the small bell three times for the commencement of meditation.

Bell-ringer: Ring the meditation bell at three-minute intervals, spreading the mat and bowing once after each stroke: the mat must be picked up and folded each time: before the first stroke, spread the mat and bow three times, and, after the last stroke, spread the mat and bow three times.

Precentor: At the end of the meditation period, clap the wooden blocks.

All: Make monjin, take the Kesa and place it upon the head.

Precentor: Lead the recitation of the Kesa verse.

All: Recite the Kesa verse with the precentor as follows

All

How great and wondrous are the clothes of enlightenment,
Formless and embracing every treasure;
I wish to unfold the Buddha's teaching
That I may help all living things.

All: Remove the Kesa from the head, touch it to the Third Eye and put it on: place the mat, folded, in front of you.

Precentor: Ring the signal gong twice.

All: Turn round clockwise and seat yourself comfortably facing outwards, with the mat again folded in front of you.

Chaplain and assistant chaplain: Leave your seat and stand in the usual place for ceremonies.

Sacristan: Turn on the heavenly canopy over the bowing seat: prepare one long, lighted stick of incense and the Three Treasures tray with powdered incense and lighted charcoal in the usual way: if the celebrant is not the abbot put down the purple bowing seat.

Acolytes: Hand the lighted incense stick and the Three Treasures tray to the chaplains in the usual way.

Chaplain and assistant chaplain: Collect the incense stick and tray from the acolytes in the usual way and return to stand in the customary places.

Celebrant (either the abbot or the master of the day if there has been a previous arrangement for the latter to do the ceremony): Leave your seat and walk on to the bowing seat, holding lotus sceptre.

Precentor: Ring the signal gong for three bows.

Celebrant: Spread the mat fully and make three full bows.

All: Make three bows with the celebrant sitting in place, the head touching the folded mat with each bow.

Precentor: Strike the large gong for the incense offering: throughout the ceremony strike the large gong at the usual places for incense offerings marked in the Scriptures by asterisks, and the small gong at the crosses indicating the end of Scriptures.

Celebrant: Walk to the incense altar in the usual way: give silent thanks for the explanation of how to train that is given in the first two Scriptures of this ceremony and make the wish that all shall understand it: offer incense, both stick and powdered, in the usual way and return to bowing seat.

Chaplain and assistant chaplain: Assist with the incense offering in the usual way.

Chaplain: Place chair on bowing seat if celebrant desires it.

Precentor: Intone the following

Precentor

Sandō - kai *

15

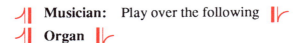
Organ

Tone II, ending 2.

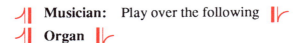 **Community**

From west | to east, unseen, flowed out the Mind of India's greatest | Sage :

And to the source kept true as an unsullied | stream is clear. ||

Although by wit and dullness the True Way is | varied, :

Yet it has no Patriarch of | south or north. ||

Here born, we clutch at | things :

And then compound delusion, later on, by | following ideals; ||

Each sense gate and * its object all together enter thus in mutual re|lations :

And yet stand apart in a uniqueness of their own, — depending and yet | non-depending both. ||

In form and feel component things are seen to differ | deeply; :

Thus are voices, in inherent iso|lation, soft or harsh. ||

Such words as high and middle darkness | match; :

Light separates the | murky from the pure. ||

The properties of the four elements together | draw :

Just as a child re|turns unto its mother. ||

Lo! — The heat of fire, — the moving wind, — the
    water wet, — the earth all | solid; :

Eyes to see, — sounds heard and smells; — upon the
    tongue the | sour, salty taste. ||

And yet, in each related thing, — as leaves grow from
    the | roots, :

End and beginning here return unto the source — and
    "high" and "low" are | used respectively. ||

Within all light is | darkness :

But explained it cannot be by darkness that one-|sided
    is alone. ||

In darkness there is | light :

But, here again, by light one-sided | it is not explained. ||

* Light goes with | darkness :

As the sequence does of | steps in walking; ||

All things herein have inherent, great potenti|ality, :

Both function, | rest, reside within. ||

Lo! — With the ideal comes the | actual, :

Like a box all | with its lid; ||

Lo! — With the ideal comes the | actual, :

Like two arrows in mid-|air that meet. ||

Completely understand here|in :

17

* The basic Truth with|in these words; ‖

† Lo! — Hear! — Set up not | your own standards. ‖

If, from your experience of the senses, — basic Truth you do not | know, :

How can you ever find the path that certain is, — no matter how far | distant you may walk? ‖

As you walk on distinctions between near and far are | lost :

And, — should you lost become, — there will arise + obstructing | mountains and great rivers. ‖

This + I offer to the seeker of great | Truth, :

Do | not waste time. ‖

Precentor

The Most Excellent Mirror—Sam - ā - dhi *

Organ

Tone VII, ending 1.

18

Community

The | Buddhas and the Ancestors have all directly handed down this | basic Truth:– :

Preserve well for you now | have; this is all. ||

The white snow falls upon the | silver plate, :

The snowy heron | in the bright moon hides; ||

Resembles each the other yet these two are | not the same; :

Combining them we can distinguish | one from other. ||

Supreme mind, — * in words, — can | never be expressed :

And yet to all the trainees' | needs it does respond; ||

Enslaved by words you fall in|to a hole. :

If you should go <u>against</u> the basic Truth — you come | to a dead-end. ||

This is as if a | giant fire-ball; :

Never come too close — nor put yourself | too far away. ||

If you ex|press by fancy words :

It | is all stained. ||

The night en|closes brightness :

And, at dawn, no | light shines; ||

This Truth holds for | beings all; :

Through this we free our|selves from suffering. ||

Although not | made by artifice, :

This Truth can find expression in the words of | those who teach true Zen. ||

It is as if one looks into a | jewelled mirror :

Seeing both shad|ow and substance. ||

You | are not him; :

He is | all of you. ||

A baby of this | world is such as this, :

Possessing all his five sense organs, — yet goes not and
neither comes, — neither arises nor yet stays, —
has words and | yet no words. ||

Then finally we | grasp nothing :

For words in|accurate will be. ||

When stacked, six | sticks of ri :

For ever move in mutual relations in ex|tremes and
centre; ||

Stacked | three times, :

Return again to the first pattern | after changes five. ||

This as the five tastes | of the chi-grass seems :

And as the diamond | sceptre's branches five. ||

The absolute "upright" holds, | as it is, :

Many phenomena within its | own delicate balance. ||

When a trainee | asks a question :

Matching answer always comes | from the Zen master. ||

So that he may bring the trainee to the | ultimate of
Truth :

The master | uses skillful means. ||

Trainees em|brace the ultimate, :

Mast|ers contain the means; ||

Cor|rectly blended, :

| This is good. ||

Avoid one-|sided clinging; :

This is all the natural and superior Truth — that does
attach itself to no delusion | or enlightenment. ||

It calmly, clearly shows when all con|ditions ripen; :

When minute infinitesimally small becomes; — when
large it transcends | all dimension, space; ||

† Even the slightest twitch will surely | break the rhythm. ||

Now we have abrupt and slow — and separated do the
sects become by setting up of | doctrines, practices, :

And these become the standards that we know of all
re|ligious conduct. ||

Even should we penetrate these | doctrines, practices, :

And then delusive consciousness flows through the
'ternal Truth, — no | progress shall we make. ||

If outwardly all calm we do appear — and yet within
dis|turbed should be :

We are as if a tethered horse — or as a | mouse within
a cage. ||

So, — | pitying this plight, :

The former sages | teaching all dispensed. ||

Because delusions in the trainees' minds were | topsy-
turvy, :

All the sages true did match there|to their teachings; ||

Thus they used all | means, so varied, :

Even so to | say that black was white. ||

Delusive thought, if | lost, abandoned, :

Will all | satisfaction bring; ||

If you in ancient | footsteps wish to walk :

Ob|serve examples old. ||

That He could take the final step to | true enlightenment, :

A former Buddha trained Himself for ten long kalpas —
gazing | at the Bodhi tree. ||

* If thus restrained, | freedom original :

Is like a tiger that has tattered ears — or | like a hobbled
horse. ||

The sage will tell a trainee, who is feeling he is low
and | all inferior, :

That on his head there gleams a jewelled diadem, —
and on his body rich robes hang — and at his feet
there | is a footrest. ||

If the trainee hears * this teaching | with surprise and
doubt, :

The sage assures him that of cats there are some kinds, —
as also some white cows, — that perfect are | just
as they are. ||

A master archer hits a target at a hundred yards because
he | skill possesses :

But, to make to meet two arrows in mid-air, — head-
on, — goes far beyond the skill of | ordinary man. ||

In this superior activity of | no-mind, :

See! the wooden figure sings — and the stone-|maiden
dances; ||

This is far beyond all | common consciousness, :
Be|yond all thinking. ||
The retainer serves his | lord the emperor; :
His father | does the child obey; ||
Without obedience there is no | filial piety :
And, if there is no | service, no advice. ||
Such action and most unpre|tentious work :
All | foolish seem + and dull ||
But those who practise thus this law + continually
    shall, | in all worlds, :
Be called Lord of Lords un|to eternity. ||

Celebrant: Go to main altar and offer incense in the usual way, when the community begins to chant each Scripture, and again at the asterisks towards the end of each Scripture when signalled to do so by the precentor.

Precentor: Sing the following offertory

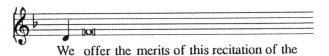

We offer the merits of this recitation of the

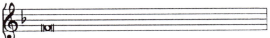

Sandōkai and *The Most Excellent*

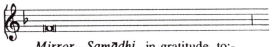

Mirror—Samādhi, in gratitude, to:-

Community

* **B**ibashibutsu Daioshō,

* Shikibutsu Daioshō,

* Bishafubutsu Daioshō,

* Kurusonbutsu Daioshō,

* Kunagonmunibutsu Daioshō,

* Kashōbutsu Daioshō,

* Shakyamunibutsu Daioshō,

Makakashyo Daioshō,

Ananda Daioshō,

Shōnawashyu Daioshō,

Ubakikuta Daioshō,

Daitaka Daioshō,

Mishaka Daioshō,

Bashumitsu Daioshō,

Butsudanandai Daioshō,

Fudamitta Daioshō,

Barishiba Daioshō,

Funayashya Daioshō,

Anabotei Daioshō,

Kabimora Daioshō,

Nagyaarajyuna Daioshō,

Kanadaiba Daioshō,

Ragorata Daioshō,

Sōgyanandai Daioshō,

Kayashyata Daioshō,

Kumorata Daioshō,

Shyyata Daioshō,

Bashyubanzu Daioshō,

Manura Daioshō,

Kakurokuna Daioshō,

Shishibodai Daioshō,

Bashyashita Daioshō,

Funyomitta Daioshō,

Hannyatara Daioshō,

Bodaidaruma Daioshō,

Taisō Eka Daiosho,

Kanchi Sōsan Daiosho,

Daiī Dōshin Daiosho,

Daiman Kōnin Daiosho,

Daikan Enō Daiosho,

Seigen Gyoshi Daiosho,

Sekitō Kisenn Daiosho,

Yakusan Igen Daiosho,

Ungan Donjyo Daiosho,

Tōzan Ryokai Daiosho,

Ungo Dōyō Daiosho,

Dōan Dōhi Daiosho,

Dōan Kanshi Daiosho,

Ryozan Enkan Daiosho,

Daiyō Kyogen Daiosho,

Tōsu Gisei Daiosho,

Fuyō Dōkai Daiosho,

Tanka Shijyun Daiosho,

Chōrō Seiryo Daiosho,

Tendō Sōkaku Daiosho,

Setchō Chikan Daiosho,

Tendō Nyojyo Daiosho,

Eihei Kōsō Daiosho,

Kōun Ejyō Daiosho,

Tettsu Gikai Daioshō,

Keizan Jōkin Daioshō,

Meihō Sotetsu Daioshō,

Shugan Dōchin Daioshō,

Tetsuzan Shikaku Daioshō,

Keigan Eishō Daioshō,

Chuzan Ryohun Daioshō,

Gisan Tōnin Daioshō,

Shōgaku Kenryu Daioshō,

Kinen Hōryu Daioshō,

Teishitsu Chisenn Daioshō,

Kokei Shōjun Daioshō,

Sessō Yūhō Daioshō,

Kaiten Genju Daioshō,

Shūzan Shunshō Daioshō,

Chōzan Senyetsu Daioshō,

Fukushū Kōchi Daioshō,

Meidō Yūton Daioshō,

Hakuhō Gentekki Daioshō,

Gesshū Sōkō Daioshō,

Manzan Dōhaku Daioshō,

Gekkan Gikō Daioshō,

Daiyu Esshō Daioshō,

Kegon Sōkai Daioshō,

Shōun Taizui Daioshō,

Nichirin Tōgō Daioshō,

Sonnō Kyodō Daioshō,

Sogaku Reidō Daioshō,

Daishun Bengyu Daioshō,

Kohō Hakugun Daioshō,

Keidō Chisan Daioshō.

Precentor

We pray that we may be able to show our

gratitude to the Four Benefactors,

rescue all beings in the Three Worlds

and make the Four Wisdoms perfect together

with all living things.

We pray that this priestly family may prosper

and all misfortune cease.

Organ and community

* Homage to all the Buddhas in all worlds,

* Homage to all the Bodhisattvas in all worlds,

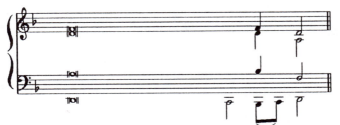

* Homage to the Scripture of Great Wis – dom.

Celebrant: Offer incense as is usual during the recitation of *The Three Homages*.

Chaplain: Remove chair.

Precentor: Ring signal gong for final three bows.

Celebrant: Make three full bows on the bowing seat: pick up and fold mat.

All: Make three bows sitting in place as at the beginning of the ceremony.

Precentor: When celebrant is ready, ring signal gong twice for trainees to get up from their seats.

All: Stand in front of places ready for the procession to the ceremony hall for morning service.

MORNING SERVICE.

Sacristan: Light candles at all shrines in the ceremony hall: turn on the heavenly canopy over the bowing seat: if the celebrant is not the abbot, put down the purple bowing seat: prepare Three Treasures tray with powdered incense and lighted charcoal: prepare one long, lighted stick of incense.

Bell-ringers: Be ready to ring the bells for morning service: start to ring when the precentor rings the signal gong twice at the end of morning office for trainees to rise from their seats.

Precentor: At the start of the second ring-down of the bells, lead the head novice's procession to the ceremony hall, ringing the signal gong in the usual way for a procession.

Head novice's procession: Head novice, head novice's assistant, then all novices in reverse seniority order: seniors follow the novices, again in reverse seniority order: postulants go from the gaitan around the outside to the ceremony hall and take their places there: all trainees take their places for morning service, the senior officers in the back rows and the rest of the community in the front and second rows: all should be in place by the time the celebrant arrives.

Assistant disciplinarian: Go to the drums and gongs and sit down.

Two acolytes: Stand ready, in the usual

places, with lighted incense stick and Three Treasures tray.

Celebrant: Wearing white robe, formal robe, Kesa and carrying mat and lotus sceptre, enter the ceremony hall after the community, either from the meditation hall or from the abbot's vestry: walk straight to the bowing seat.

Chaplain and assistant chaplain: Follow the celebrant: go to usual places: collect lighted incense stick and tray from the acolytes in the usual way and return to places.

Assistant disciplinarian: Ring the signal gong for three bows.

Celebrant: Spread mat fully and make three bows.

Community except chaplains: Spread mat, folded, and make three bows with celebrant: pick up mats and place them, folded, on seats with the small triangles on the underside towards the front of the seat: sit down.

Congregation: Make three seated bows.

Assistant disciplinarian: Strike the large gong for the first incense offering and, thereafter, strike the large and small gongs at the usual places throughout the ceremony.

Celebrant: Go to altar: silently give thanks for another day in which to train and for the Scriptures which tell us how to do it, especially *The Scripture of Great Wisdom:* offer stick and powdered incense in the usual way and return to bowing seat.

Chaplain and assistant chaplain: Assist with incense offering in the usual way: return to places.

Chaplain: Place chair on bowing seat, if desired, by the celebrant.

Chaplain and assistant chaplain: Spread mats, folded, and make three bows: place mats, folded, on seats and sit down.

Precentor: Intone the following

Precentor

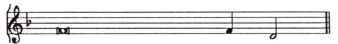

The   Scripture   of   Great   Wis - dom *

Musician: Play over the following

Organ

Tone III, ending 1.

All

When one | with deepest | wisdom of the heart :
    That is beyond dis|criminative thought, ||
The Holy Lord, — great | Kanzeon Bosatsu, :
Knew that the skandhas five were, — as they are, —
    in their self-nature, — | void, unstained and pure. ||
O Shariputra, | form is only pure, :
Pure is all form; there | is, then, nothing more than this, ||

For what is form is pure — and | what * is pure is form; :

The same is also true of all sensation, — thought, ac|tivity and consciousness. ||

O Shariputra, | here all things are pure :

For they are neither | born nor do they wholly die; ||

They are not stained nor | yet immaculate; :

In|creasing not, decreasing not. ||

O Shariputra, — in this pure there is no form, — sensation, — thought, — activity or | consciousness; :

No eye, — ear, — nose, — tongue, — body, — mind; — no form, — no tastes, — sound, — | colour, touch or objects; ||

Vision none; — no consciousness; — no knowledge and no | sign of ignorance; :

Until we come to where old age and death have ceased — and so has all ex|tinction of old age and death ||

For here there is no suffering, — nor yet again is there ac|cumulation, :

Nor again annihilation nor an Eightfold Path, — no | knowledge, no attainment. ||

In the mind of the Bosatsu who is truly one with Wisdom Great the | obstacles dissolve :

* And, — going on beyond this human | mind, he IS Nirvana. ||

All the Buddhas True of present, — past and | future they ARE all, :

34

Because upon Great Wisdom they rely, — the
    perfect | and most high enlightenment. ||
The Prajnaparamita one should know — to be the
    Greatest | Mantra of them all, :
The highest and most peerless Mantra too; —
    * allayer | of all pain Great Wisdom is, ||
It is the very | Truth, no falsehood here. :
This is the | Mantra of Great Wisdom, hear! ||
+ O Buddha, going, going, | going on + beyond :
And always going on beyond, — always
    BECOMING | Buddha. Hail! Hail! Hail! ||

Celebrant: Offer incense at the usual
places indicated in the Scripture by
asterisks.
Precentor: Intone the following offertory

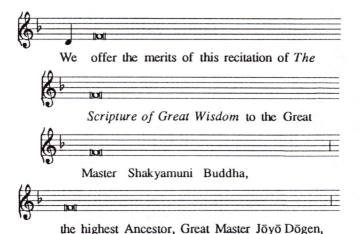

We   offer the merits of this recitation of *The*

Scripture of Great Wisdom to the Great

Master Shakyamuni Buddha,

the highest Ancestor, Great Master Jōyō Dōgen,

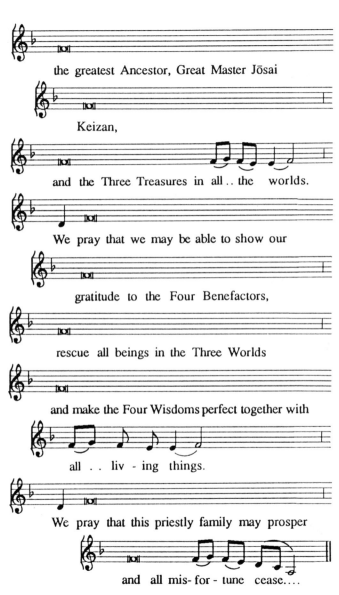

the greatest Ancestor, Great Master Jōsai

Keizan,

and the Three Treasures in all .. the worlds.

We pray that we may be able to show our

gratitude to the Four Benefactors,

rescue all beings in the Three Worlds

and make the Four Wisdoms perfect together with

all .. liv - ing things.

We pray that this priestly family may prosper

and all mis- for - tune cease....

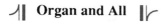

Organ and All

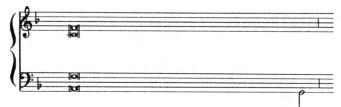

* Homage to all the Buddhas in all worlds,

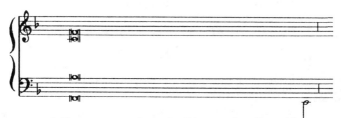

* Homage to all the Bodhisattvas in all worlds,

* Homage to the Scripture of Great Wis – dom.

FOUNDER'S CEREMONY.

Celebrant: Wear the same formal robe and Kesa and carry the same mat and lotus sceptre as were used for the ceremony hall part of morning service.

Musician: Have prepared *The Litany of the Great Compassionate One,* the *Adoration of the Buddha's Relics* and *The Three Homages:* come in as appropriate during the ceremony.

Sacristan: During the recitation of the *Homages* at the end of the ceremony hall morning service, light all candles and lights in the Founder's Shrine except those in front of the memorial tablets of former members of the community: prepare powdered incense box with lighted charcoal in front of the main altar of the Founder's Shrine and stand it on an incense altar.

Acolyte: Light and carry two long incense sticks, to be received by the chaplain, in the same way as you would for a memorial ceremony.

Chaplain: Receive two lighted incense sticks from the acolyte to the celebrant's right of the altar in the usual way and bring them to the celebrant.

Celebrant: Do not return to the bowing seat after *The Three Homages* at the end of morning service: wait in front of main altar to receive one incense stick from the chaplain.

Chaplain: At the end of *The Three Homages* hand one of the two incense sticks to the celebrant in the usual way.

Celebrant: Offer incense stick to the Founder of the temple whilst making the wish that all may find the Eternal and that the Founder may for ever be watching over the temple and, especially, the abbot with silent eyes: offer powdered incense in the usual way: turn to the left and walk round the main altar to the Founder's Shrine.

Chaplain: Carrying the second incense stick, walk round the right side of the altar to meet the celebrant at the door of the Founder's Shrine and follow him inside.

Precentor: Intone the following whilst the celebrant is offering the first stick of incense and making his wish

Precentor

The Litany of the Great Compassionate One *

Musician: Play over the following

All: Chant the following

Adoration to the Triple | Treasure! :
Adoration to Kanzeon Who is the Great
Com|passionate One! ||

Om to the One Who leaps beyond all | fear! :

Having adored Him, — may I enter into the heart of the
Noble, | Adored Kanzeon! ||

His life is the completion of | meaning; :

It is pure, — it is that which makes all beings
victorious — and cleanses the | path of all
existence. ||

Om, — O Thou Seer, — World-tran|scending One! :

O hail to the | Great Bodhisattva! ||

All, — all is defilement, defilement, earth, | earth. :

Do, do the | work within my heart. ||

O great Victor, I hold on, hold | on! :

To Indra the Cre|ator I cry! ||

Move, move, my defilement-|free One! :

Come, come, hear, hear, a | joy springs up in me! ||

Speak, speak, give me di|rection! :

Awakened, awakened, | I have awakened! ||

O merciful One, com|passionate One, :

Of daring ones the | most joyous, hail! ||

Thou art all suc|cessful, hail! :

Thou art the great suc|cessful One, hail! ||

Thou hast attained mastery in the | discipline, hail! :

Thou hast a weapon with|in Thine hand, hail! ||
Thou hast the Wheel within Thine | hand, hail! :
Thou Who | hast the lotus, hail! ||
Hail to Thee Who art the root of e|ternity! :
Hail to Thee Who | art all compassion! Hail! ||
Adoration to the Triple | Treasure! Hail! :
Give ear unto | this my prayer, hail! ||

Assistant disciplinarian: Ring the large gong at the usual asterisks in *The Litany of the Great Compassionate One:* ring the end of the first incense offering as the celebrant gets to the corner of the main altar to go to the Founder's Shrine.

Two acolytes: Stand in the corners on either side of the doors in the Founder's Shrine: as the celebrant steps through the door spread mats, folded, and make three full bows: thereafter stand in gasshō during the entire ceremony.

Celebrant: Enter the Founder's Shrine by the centre of the doorway with the left foot first: walk on the bowing seat, putting the left foot first, and go directly to the main altar.

Chaplain: Hand the remaining stick of incense in the usual way to the celebrant.

Celebrant: Offer the incense stick in the usual way whilst making the wish that the Eternal, Founder and Ancestors shall help with all decisions throughout that day, owing to the recognition within oneself of one's humanity, weaknesses and fallibility:

thereafter offer powdered incense in the usual way: return to the bottom of the bowing seat in the usual way: spread the mat fully and make three bows, offering submission to the guidance of the Eternal, the Founder and the Ancestors as well as asking for help in every matter with each bow: also give thanks for the fact that they appeared in this world to give help with each bow and allow gratitude for this to pour forth as each bow is made: at the end of the bows stand, pick up and fold the mat and make monjin on the bowing seat: turn clockwise, step off the bowing seat with the left foot, walk boldly through the centre of the door, stepping out of the shrine with the left foot, and return to the front of the main altar of the ceremony hall via the opposite side from which you went to the Founder's Shrine: on arrival in front of the main altar take two side steps in front of the incense altar and make the second powdered incense offering of *The Litany of the Great Compassionate One* when the gong sounds: side step back to your right side of the incense altar, turn towards the bowing seat and walk to the bottom of it, making certain that the number of steps taken corresponds with one of the numbers of teachings of the Buddha: on arrival at the bottom of the bowing seat step on with the left foot: spread the mat fully on the bowing seat.

Chaplain: Do not make the three bows with the celebrant: follow him out of the shrine then go to stand in your usual place without going to the main altar.

Assistant disciplinarian: Do not ring for the second incense offering, even if it happens to be late, until the celebrant gets back in front of the incense altar in front of the main altar: ring for the end of the second incense offering when he arrives back on the bowing seat with both feet. Ring the small gong at the crosses shewn at the end of *The Litany of the Great Compassionate One* to signal its end.

Precentor: Intone the following which is chanted to the end and repeated for the first few lines ending with "for our present body."

Precentor

Adoration of the Buddha's Re - lics *

Organ and all

Hom--age to... the... Re----lics of the Budd--ha of

43

mer-----it.....all; Hom----age to the Bod--y

of Truth which is Truth It--self....and a Stup--a for

the World of the Dhar--ma for our pres--ent bod--y.

Through the mer--its of the Budd--ha   the Truth

en--ters in--to us and we en--ter the Truth; through the

ex--cell--ent pow--er of Budd--ha we real--ize Truth.

Let us do on--ly good things for all liv--ing things

that we may poss--ess the true... Mind; let us do

on--ly pure deeds...... that we may en--ter the

peace------ful Mind which is un-chang----ing Great

Wis--dom; Let us pay hom-----age e--ter--nal--ly

to the Budd--ha, to the Budd--ha, to the Budd--ha.

Celebrant: Offer incense in the usual way at the places indicated by the asterisks in the Scripture and signalled by the assistant disciplinarian on the large gong.

Assistant disciplinarian: Signal on the large gong for the celebrant to begin the two incense offerings during the *Adoration of the Buddha's Relics* at the first asterisk (at the start of the Scripture on the word "Homage" and on the same word "Homage" when it is repeated): signal the end of the two offerings when the celebrant again arrives with both feet on the bowing seat or, if no celebrant, at the second asterisk: signal the end of the Scripture, ringing the small gong twice in close succession, at the crosses (when the repeated section is recited at the end only).

Precentor: Recite the following offertory

Precentor

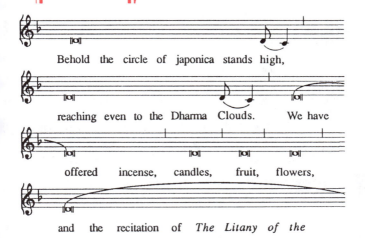

Behold the circle of japonica stands high,

reaching even to the Dharma Clouds. We have

offered incense, candles, fruit, flowers,

and the recitation of *The Litany of the*

Great Compassionate One and the *Adoration of the Buddha's Relics* to the Buddha Keidō Chi- -san Kō- -hō, Found - er of this monastery; who showed the Truth from the time of our True Master Shakyakmuni to that of our Master to this ver - y day.

May the offerings we make here show our gratitude and joy to all liv-- ing things. We pray that the merits thereof shall not only be giv - en

to our Found-- er, but . . . . light the way

of all who have not yet found the . . Truth.

Organ and all

* Homage to all the Buddhas in all worlds,

* Homage to all the Bodhisattvas in all worlds,

* Homage to the Scripture of Great Wis – dom.

Chaplain: Remove chair.

Assistant chaplain: Remove tray.

Precentor: Ring the signal gong for the three bows.

All: Make three bows as is usual, community with folded mats.

Precentor: Ring the signal gong for all to make monjin to main altar.

All: Make monjin to main altar.

Precentor: Ring the signal gong for all to make monjin to each other.

All: Make monjin to each other with clasped hands.

Celebrant: Make standing bow with hands open, lotus sceptre held in usual way: turn clockwise and walk to the centre back of the ceremony hall, stepping off the bowing seat with the left foot: turn clockwise and face altar, standing between the two chaplains, but two steps in front of them, facing the altar.

Precentor: When celebrant turns to walk down the bowing seat, walk to centre back of ceremony hall: face the altar, between the chaplains, but five steps further back than they are. Ring the signal gong for final bow.

All except celebrant: Make monjin with clasped hands.

Celebrant: Make monjin with hands open, lotus sceptre in left hand and tassels in right.

Precentor: Proceed to the far side of the assistant chaplain, ringing the signal gong.

Celebrant: Follow precentor.

Chaplains: Follow the celebrant.

Celebrant's recession: Precentor, celebrant, chaplain and assistant chaplain recess to the abbot's vestry: celebrant and chaplains enter: precentor makes monjin in the doorway whilst ringing the signal gong twice.

Community: Recess to the meditation hall in the usual way and stand in front of your places until the assistant disciplinarian, or precentor, rings the signal gong for the three gratitude bows.

Precentor or assistant disciplinarian Ring signal gong for three gratitude bows.

All: Make three gratitude bows.

SCRIPTURAL RECITATION FOR
THE LORD OF THE KITCHEN STOVE.

Special note: When the chief cook has made his selection of the rice and vegetables for the day [choben: made up the menu] around ten o'clock, he has his acolyte (Anja) do the Scriptural Recitation for the Lord of the Kitchen Stove. He offers incense and the acolyte recites *The Litany of the Great Compassionate One* (found on page 39) and does the transfer of merit or offertory. (In a small temple it can be done after morning services.)

Offertory

We offer the merits of this recitation of *The Litany of the Great Compassionate One* to the Guardian Deity, the Lord of the Kitchen Stove for our temple, that He may protect the Dharma and set monks' minds at ease.

All

Homage to all the Buddhas in all worlds,
Homage to all the Bodhisattvas in all worlds,
Homage to *The Scripture of Great Wisdom.*

DINING HALL CEREMONIAL AND ABRIDGED PROCEDURE FOR FOOD ALTAR.

Special note: When formal breakfast is abridged, a food altar is arranged by the kitchen, places are provided in the dining hall for the community, an incense altar is set out in the median, all as according to the following diagram (fig. 1). The use of signal instruments is done in conformity with the prescribed method. The abbot and others take their seats according to seniority. Following the signals struck with the mallet or the clappers, the mealtime verses are chanted as monks set out their bowls and utensils. (The begging bowl is not used.) Food is served, the food offering made and the meal eaten. The meal ends in the usual way with the recitation of the closing verse ("The universe is…") and the monks' processional including the three gratitude bows. When abridging the ceremony, the clappers (taku) are struck once and the community assembles. The drum roll is omitted. The recitations are done following the lead of the clappers, bowl sets are opened, food is served and a food offering is made. Once the meal is eaten, the usual closing of the meal is done along with its recitation and then the monks recess from the hall.

Offertory

We offer the merits of this recitation of the mealtime Scriptures to the Guardian Deity, the Lord of the Kitchen Stove for our temple, that He may protect the Dharma and set monks' minds at ease.

⫞ All ⫞

Homage to all the Buddhas in all worlds,
Homage to all the Bodhisattvas in all worlds,
Homage to *The Scripture of Great Wisdom.*

Diagram for Abridged Procedure for Food Altar.

A = Visiting Monastic Dignitaries
B = Inō: Precentor
C = Fūsu: Assistant Supervisory Officer in Charge of Revenue and Expenditures
D = Shōko: Abbot's Incense Chaplain
E = Shojō: Abbot's Secretarial Chaplain
F = Ehatsu: Abbot's Robe- and Bowl-handling Chaplain
G = Tōyaku: Abbot's Food Chaplain
H = Hanjū: Monk in Charge of the Rice
I = Shōkyaku: Abbot's Guest-handling Chaplain
J = Shissui: Extern Sacristan
K = Tenzo: Chief Cook
L = Kansu: Supervisory Officer
M = Tsūsu: Chief Supervisory Officer
N = Shuso: Head Novice
O = Shoki: Clerical Officer
P = Chizō: Chief Librarian
Q = Chiyoku: Bath Monk
R = Kakudō: Monk in Charge of Visiting Monastic Dignitaries
S = Ka'an: Guestmaster's Assistant
T = Dōan: Assistant Disciplinarian
U = Chiden: Officer in Charge of the Ceremony Hall
V = Shika: Guestmaster
W = Jishō: Attendant on the Sacred Images in the Meditation Hall
X = Jishin: Sacristan
Y = Godō: Chief Lecturer
Z = Jōnin: Servers
✿ = Other Monks of the Community

fig. 1

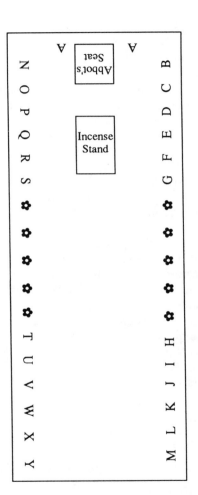

SHURANGAMA CEREMONY.

Community: Process into ceremony hall taking positions as shown in fig. 2 on page 74. Monks face altar. Precentor and chief reciter stand on right and left side of bowing seat respectively.

Abbot's procession: Abbot or representative, carrying fountain sceptre, goes to bowing seat and offers incense in usual way assisted by chaplains. Upon returning the chaplains take their places in row directly behind and on each side of bowing seat.

Assistant disciplinarian: After abbot returns to bowing seat signal three bows.

Community: Make three bows, full mat. Pick up mats, then the row nearest altar turns clockwise and faces second row; the third row turns clockwise to face last row. Those monks in line on north side turn and face bowing seat. Precentor and reciter face each other.

Precentor: Intone the following

Precentor

A doration to the Buddhas and Bodhisattvas assembled for the Shurangama Festival

Precentor: Recite the following

Precentor

*T*he Shurangama Litany *

Community: Recite the following

◀| Community |▶

At that time the World-honoured One, from the fleshy crown of His head, sent out a sparkling flood of light rays and, amidst these rays, burst forth a thousand-petaled jewelled lotus.

A transformed Tathagata sat within this jewelled flower the crown of His head emitting hundreds of glistening light rays in all directions;

Everywhere each light revealed all things as numerous as the myriad grains of sand in the Ganges.

The Vajrapanis, Jewel in hand, lighted up the mountains, appearing everywhere within the vault of space; the great assembly beheld this with awe.

Unable to hold on to their fears and desires, they sought the Buddha's pity and aid and wholeheartedly hearkened unto the radiant Tathagata atop the now-concealed crown of the Buddha's head as He chanted this sacred Invocation.

◀| **Precentor:** Recite the following |▶

◀| **Precentor** |▶

The Invocation of All the Transformations of the Invincible One *

Assistant disciplinarian: After Invocation is intoned, ring signal gong for monks to bow, ring again to turn in appropriate direction and a third ring to begin circumambulation. After *The Scripture of Great Wisdom* has begun and monks have returned to starting positions, ring signal gong once for rows to turn and face each other as in the beginning, and ring again to bow.

Community: Recite the following whilst doing the special circumambulation for this ceremony. Circumambulate until *The Scripture of Great Wisdom* begins. The assistant disciplinarian will give usual signals to begin and end.

Abbot, precentor and reciter: Move into third row for circumambulation. Return to starting positions at end of circumambulation.

Community

Homage to all the Buddhas and Bodhisattvas!
Homage to the Seven Fully Enlightened Buddhas and to their disciples within the billions of sanghas!
Homage to the realm of the Arahants!
Homage to those who have entered the stream!
Homage to those who are to be reborn but once more!
Homage to those who will not be reborn again!
Homage to the realm of the completely successful One who practises right actions!
Homage to the Triple Treasure!

Homage to the exalted Lord who conquers with His resolute host of celestial warriors, the Tathagata, the Arahant, the Fully Enlightened One!
Homage to the exalted Amitábha, the One of Infinite Light, the Tathagata, the Arahant, the Fully Enlightened One!
Homage to the exalted Aksobháya, the Immutable One, the Tathagata, the Arahant, the Fully Enlightened One!

Homage to the exalted Bhaisájya-guru, Radiant Healing Lord of the Indestructible Lapis Lazuli, the Tathagata, the Arahant, the Fully Enlightened One!

Homage to the exalted Shaléndra, Lord of the Most Excellent of Sala Trees in Full Bloom, the Tathagata, the Arahant, the Fully Enlightened One!

Homage to the exalted Shakyamuni, the Tathagata, the Arahant, the Fully Enlightened One!

Homage to the exalted Rátnakúsumakétu, Lord of the Flowering Jewel Banner which is the standard for our vow to train, the Tathagata, the Arahant, the Fully Enlightened One!

Homage to the exalted Family of the Tathagata!

Homage to the exalted Family of the Lotus!

Homage to the exalted Family of the Vajra-diamond!

Homage to the exalted Family of the Mani-jewel!

Homage to the exalted Family of Action blossoming forth from the Water of the Spirit!

Homage to the wise and holy ones who live amidst the devas!

Homage to those who preserve these words of pure and bright Dharma!

Homage to the wise and holy ones who preserve this pure Dharma and to those who likewise facilitate Its recitation!

Homage to Brahma who is the yearning of the heart!

Homage to Indra who is the will to train!

Homage to the exalted Rudra, the Wrathful and Purifying One, companion to Uma, the One Who Brings True Peace!

Homage to Narayána of the five great mudra seals, along with His guardians!

Homage to the Adored One!

Homage to Mahakála, Him of the Dark Realms, who put to flight the triply-fortified cities of the haughty asuras, the Confident One, along with His host of Divine Mothers who dwell within the burning-grounds of the dead!

Homage to the Adored One!

* We bow in homage to all of You for You are the white canopy of light that covers the crown of the exalted Tathagata's head, all the Transformations of the Invincible One adored by all celestial beings, honoured by all celestial beings and guarded over by every celestial being!

We pray that You make all devilish entanglements and fascinations subside,

Make known what needs to be known,

Tame those who would prolong pain,

Protect us from evil,.

Keep us safe from an untimely death,

Liberate us from all our fetters,

Protect us from all that is difficult to tame and from nightmarish dreams,

Free us from the four and eighty thousand enticements,

Purify the eight and twenty mansions wherein the Moon of our Original Nature abides,

Rid us of the eight great distractions of gain and loss, fame and disgrace, praise and ridicule, elation and sorrow,

Protect us from all enemies,

Make all mysteries disappear and evil visions dissolve
And make us strangers to poison, sword, fire and flood.

We call upon Thee, the Great Fierce One from the Family of the Invincible, the Great Adítya whose mighty brilliance blazes forth like the sun, destroying all darkness,

And upon Thee, the Great Dazzling White One of the blazing light, the mighty white-robed One who abides within the white lotus, the Noble Liberator born from the tear-filled eye of Compassion,

And upon Thee, Bhríkuti, the Wrathful Frowning One who sprang from the scowling brow of Compassion,

And upon Thee, the victorious Vajrámriti, the Indestructible One crystal clear as the Sweet Dew,

And upon Thee, the flower-wreathed Vajra-tongued One famed for Thy teaching of the ways to sit in meditation,

And upon Thee, the One with the Invincible Vajra-sceptre, honoured by celestial beings as the One who is thoroughly free from defiling passions,

And upon Thee, Avalokiteshwára, the Great White One whose form is as a flower,

And upon Thee with the Vajra-chains which bind all evil, second only to the Noble Avalokiteshwára in might, along with Thy Vajra-handmaidens, the upholders of the Families,

And upon Thee, the Golden-garlanded One whose great knowledge is as a diamond which Thou holdest in Thy hand, the Jewel in the Red Safflower, Vairochána, from whose actions the head crown arises,

And upon Thee, Lochána, with Thy garlands in full bloom, Divine Mother Who is Wisdom, Thee whose Vajra is lustrous as gold, who, like the Vajra-beaked Garúda, swallows the serpent of hatred, the Dazzling White One whose eyes are like lotus blossoms, radiant as the moon at its fullest.

As thus we speak, may all of You through Your multitudinous mudra signs protect us from all things!

* Om to the crown of the Tathagata which the whole assembly of Holy Ones praise!

Hūm trūm, smash all fetters!

Hūm trūm, restrain all evil!

Hūm trūm, shine forth!

Hūm trūm, stir up the lethargic mind!

Hūm trūm, bestow upon us what needs to be known!

Hūm trūm, restrain all corruption and wickedness!

Hūm trūm, bring to an end all entanglements with demons that bedevil us by day or stalk us by night!

Hūm trūm, free us from the four and eighty thousand enticements!

Hūm trūm, purify the eight and twenty mansions where the Moon of our Original Nature abides!

Hūm trūm, rid us of the eight great distractions!

Protect us, we pray, protect us!

To That which transforms atop the crown of the Tathagata's head, to the Great Vajradhára, the Thousand-armed One with a thousand heads and a hundred thousand eyes, indestructible, whose radiance blazes up through the Mandala of the Three Worlds,

Om, we pray, help us to return to our Original Nature!

* By being mindful, may I be cleansed
Of fear of rulers and whatever else would dominate me,
Of fear of thieves and whatever else would rob or deprive me,
Of fear of fire and whatever else may enflame or consume me,
Of fear of flood and whatever else would overwhelm or drown me,
Of fear of poison and whatever else would corrupt me,
Of fear of weapons and whatever else may wound or maim me,
Of fear of hostile armies and whatever else may assault me,
Of fear of famine and want, and whatever else may starve or deprive me,
Of fear of lightning and whatever else may strike me suddenly and unexpectedly,
Of fear of untimely death,
Of fear of being overwhelmed by earthquakes and whatever else may shake the ground from beneath me,
Of fear of falling meteors and whatever else may befall me from the heavens,
Of fear of a ruler's rod and whatever else would inflict punishment or pain upon me,
Of fear of snakes and dragons and whatever else would crush me in its coils,
Of fear of storms and whatever else may thunder down upon me,
Of fear of vultures and eagles and whatever else would prey upon me.
By being mindful, may I be cleansed
Of entanglements with the imps of mischief and scorn,

Of entanglements with those who stalk the night,

Of entanglements with hungry ghosts,

Of entanglements with the demons of despair,

Of entanglements with the demons of deception and confusion,

Of entanglements with things that sexually fascinate,

Of entanglements with the demons of agitation and fury,

Of entanglements with the demons of neglectfulness,

Of entanglements with Skanda, lord of argument and disease,

Of entanglements with the demons who bring on twitchings,

Of entanglements with the demons of intoxication and raging desire,

Of entanglements with nightmares and shadows,

Of entanglements with Révati, she who indulges in abusiveness.

By being mindful, may I be cleansed

Of whatever would rob me of my giving rise to spiritual intentions,

Of whatever would rob me of the Child whilst It is still developing in the hara,

Of whatever would rob me of the newly born Child,

Of whatever would rob me of my vitality,

Of whatever would rob me of my blood,

Of whatever would rob me of my breath,

Of whatever would rob me of my skin,

Of whatever would rob me of my flesh,

Of whatever would rob me of my marrow,

Of whatever would rob me of my vomit,

Of whatever would rob me of my bodily excretions,

Of whatever would rob me of my mind.

By being mindful, may I be cleansed
Of all these and of all other enticements and distractions.

By being mindful of those who are homeless mendicant monks, may I be cleansed;

By being mindful of the daemons who lay bare the Truth, may I be cleansed;

By being mindful of Rudra, the Purifier who rages like a tempest, may I be cleansed;

By being mindful of the True Garúda who swallows the serpent of hate, may I be cleansed;

By being mindful of Mahakála and His host of Divine Mothers, may I be cleansed;

By being mindful of Kapálika whose skull is our begging bowl, may I be cleansed;

By being mindful of those who make us victorious, those who offer us the Divine Nectar and those who grant us the means to do all that needs to be done, may I be cleansed;

By being mindful of the Four Divine Sisters, the Transcendent Virtues that abide within the world beyond form, may I be cleansed;

By being mindful of Bríngiriti, bringer of victory, Nandikéshvara, bringer of joy, and Gánapati, clearer of paths, may I be cleansed;

By being mindful of those who are free from all ties and fetters, may I be cleansed;

By being mindful of the Arahants, may I be cleansed;

By being mindful of the excellent and distinguished assembly of monks, may I be cleansed;

By being mindful of Vajrapáni, the Bodhicitta of all the Tathagatas whose hand holds the Jewel, may I be cleansed;

By being mindful of Brahma and of Rudra and of
Narayána, may I be cleansed;

By being mindful of Guhyakádhipati, the Unseen Lord
of the Gúhyakas who guard the Treasure, may I be
cleansed.

Protect me, I pray, protect me!

* O Exalted One, I dedicate myself to Your canopy of
white light which, radiantly spreading forth from its
black stem, opens like a blossom!

Blaze up, blaze up!

Burn out our passions!

Burn away all defilements!

Cleave our bonds!

Tear our fetters asunder!

Sever our entanglements!

Bind all evil! Hūm, hūm, Peace, Peace. All Hail!

With joyous laughter we cry Peace!

To the Unfailing One, Peace!

To the Indestructible One, Peace!

To the Bestower of gifts, Peace!

To the One who puts the warring asuras to flight, Peace!

To all celestial beings, Peace!

To all nagas, Peace!

To all imps of mischief and scorn, Peace!

To all stalkers of the night, Peace!

To all who inflict suffering on those who hate, Peace!

To all who would storm the gates to the Heavens,
Peace!

To all who distract from training by singing, Peace!

To all who distract from training by playing music,
Peace!

To all who distract from training by dancing about, Peace!

To all that creates deception, Peace!

To all that disheartens through despair, Peace!

To all that arouses sexual fascination, Peace!

To all who stir things up, Peace!

To all who encourage neglectfulness, Peace!

To all who break the Precepts, Peace!

To all that is difficult to look upon, Peace!

To all that is painful and grievous, Peace!

To all that gives rise to twitchings, Peace!

To all who listen but still cleave to non-Buddhist paths, Peace!

To all manner of misguided ways, Peace!

To all forms of intoxication, Peace!

To all teachers of spiritual knowledge, Peace!

To those who make us victorious or offer us the Divine Nectar or create the means to do all that needs to be done or are teachers of spiritual knowledge, Peace!

To the Four Divine Sisters, Peace!

To the Vajra Handmaidens who uphold the Families and to the Lords of Knowledge, Peace!

To the Great Body of Transformations, Peace!

To Vajrashankára, the Beneficent Lord of Transformations, Peace!

To Mahakála, Peace!

To His host of Divine Mothers, Peace!

To the Adored One, Peace!

To Indra, warring lord against the asuras, Peace!

To the Possessor of Sacred Knowledge, Peace!

To Rudra, the Raging One, Peace!

To Vishnu, perpetuator of all phenomena, Peace!

To Brahma, creator of all phenomena, Peace!

To the one who resists, Peace!

To Agni, Wisdom's Flame which consumes all
　　ignorance and passion, Peace!

To Mahakáli, Her of the Dark Realms, Peace!

To Raúdri who follows upon Rudra as self-righteous-
　　ness and brutality follow upon rage, Peace!

To Kaladándi, wielder of the scythe of death, Peace!

To Aíndri who follows upon Indra as violence follows
　　upon warlike intentions, Peace!

To Wisdom, the Divine Mother, Peace!

To Chamúndi, weaver and severer of enchantments,
　　Peace!

To Kalarátri who brings the dark night of death, Peace!

To Kapáli who wears the necklace of skulls, Peace!

To the Confident One who dwells within the graveyard,
　　Peace!

* If there are any sentient beings

With a corrupt and malignant mind,

Or with an evil mind,

Or with a brutal and raging mind,

Or with a hostile mind

Or with an unfriendly mind,

May they give rise to this Invocation, cleanse them-
　　selves with It by speaking It aloud, praying It in
　　whispers or reading It silently

Lest they rob us of our first conception of the Truth,

Or rob us of the developing Child within the hara,

Or rob Him of His blood,

Or rob Him of His skin,

Or rob Him of His flesh,

Or rob Him of His marrow,

Or rob Him of His birth,

Or rob Him of His new life,
Or rob Him of His vitality,
Or rob Him of His talents,
Or rob Him of His innocence,
Or rob Him of His brightness,
Or rob Him of His flowering,
Or rob Him of His fruition,
Or rob Him of the harvest of His fruits,
Or if there are any
With an evil mind,
Or a malignant and corrupt mind
As a result of entanglement with a celestial being,
Or entanglement with a naga,
Or entanglement with a mischievous or malicious imp,
Or entanglement with a stalker of the night,
Or entanglement with one who is resentful or craves power,
Or entanglement with an avenger of hatred,
Or entanglement with whatever distracts training by appealing to the ear,
Or entanglement with whatever distracts training by appealing to the eye,
Or entanglement with a hungry ghost,
Or entanglement with a demon of despair,
Or entanglement with that which creates deception and confusion,
Or entanglement with one who stirs things up,
Or entanglement with an encourager of neglectfulness,
Or entanglement with that which arouses sexual fascination,
Or entanglement with Skanda, lord of argument and disease,
Or entanglement with intoxications,

Or entanglement with nightmares and shadows,

Or entanglement with what brings on convulsions, twitching and fits,

Or entanglement with whatever drains us of our vitality,

Or entanglement with those who indulge in abusiveness,

Or entanglement with those who beg from greed,

Or entanglement with birds of omen,

Or entanglement with elation over auspicious signs,

Or entanglement with hypocrites and rogues,

Or entanglement with those who strangle to extort,

Or if there are any

Who burn with a fever, such as the one-day fever, the two-day fever, the three-day fever, the four-day fever, a constant fever or a chronic fever,

Or suffer from the humour that leads to irritability, the peevishness of biliousness or the apathy of phlegm,

Or are overwhelmed to the point of collapse,

Or suffer from all manner of feverish headaches,

Or are immobilized,

Or who suffer from disgust over things indigestible,

Or whose sight is diseased,

Or whose mouth is diseased,

Or whose heart is diseased,

Or who suffer from earache, tooth-ache, heartburn, pain in some vital organ, sore joints, chest pains, back ache, stomach ache, pinched nerves, sciatica, kidney or gall stones, painful thighs, hip pain, sore hands, sore feet or pain throughout their whole body,

Or have a fever brought on by some demon who throws them into confusion or resurrects dead issues or drains their energies,

Or who suffer from things that get under the skin and itch, or fester, like scabies, ringworm, boils and abscesses, or things that create rot, like syphilis and leprosy, or things that harden like callouses or corns,

Or who are swept with nausea,

Or are wasting away with consumption,

Or meet with an accident through such things as fire and flood,

Or with an untimely death by some insect's poisonous bite or sting, or by scorpion's or serpent's venom, or within the claws and fangs of some lion, tiger, bear or hyena,

O all Ye victors over Mara who are the Transformations within the canopy of white light that streams forth from the Great Vajra Crown for ten yojanas in all directions,

Help me to restrain such entanglements with gentle kindness and friendliness,

Help me to restrain them in all the ten quarters,

Help me to restrain them with full knowledge of what needs to be done,

Help me to restrain them with dignity and in full light,

Help me to restrain them with my very hands,

Help me to restrain them with my very feet,

Help me to restrain them with my whole body and every part of it.

Thus I pray:–

Ōm to Thee, Flame of the Sweet Dew, blaze forth in all Your brilliance and purity, shine forth Your skilful tenderness!

O Vajrapáni, Heroic One, Thee who holdest the Diamond of Wisdom in Thy hand, restrain all that would fetter us! Peace!

Hūm trūm, Peace! All Hail!

Homage to the Tathagata, the Successful One, the Arahant, the Fully Enlightened One who has completely realized the Wisdom that is the Path of the Divine Mother Prajnaparamita! All Hail!

Precentor

The Scripture of Great Wisdom *

Community: Chant *The Scripture of Great Wisdom,* which is found on page 33.

Precentor: Recite the following offertory

Precentor

The community of monks assembled here before our very eyes

Have chanted the profound and subtle *Litany of the Shurangama*

And offer the merit thereof to those who defend and protect the Dharma—the nagas, the devas

And the guardian deity of this monastery which all the Holy Ones have built.

May all who are mired down in the three evil paths, or are caught in the eight difficult situations, let go of their suffering;

May the Four Benefactors and those in the Three Realms of existence to whom we are completely indebted prosper,

May all nations be at peace and warring cease,

May the winds and rain be seasonable and the people
enjoy health and happiness,
May our cultivation of practice and training progress
apace so that we may forthwith transcend the Ten
Stages of Bodhisattvahood without impediments.
May our monastery ward off all evil, stay undefiled and
be free from worries and mishaps,
May donors and believers turn their ways toward
reverence and thereby increase their blessings and
wisdom.

Community

Homage to all the Buddhas in all worlds,
Homage to all the Bodhisattvas in all worlds,
Homage to *The Scripture of Great Wisdom*.

> **Assistant disciplinarian:**   Signal three
> bows.
> **Community:**   All turn toward altar, make
> three bows with full mat.
> **Abbot:**   Make three bows, pick up mat
> and make three gratitude bows in usual way.
> **Abbot and community:**   Recess.

fig. 2

Diagram for the Shurangama Ceremony.

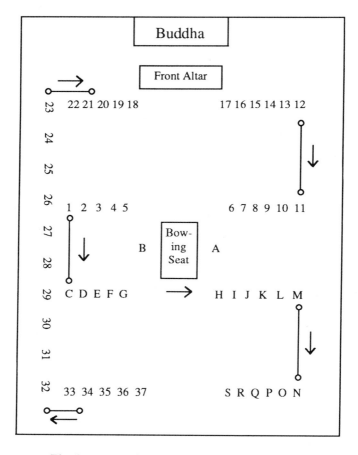

The Precentor, the Abbot and the Chief Reciter
enter the circumambulation between
the Shoki (G) and the Tsūsu (H)

A = Inō: Precentor
B = Ryōgon-tō: Chief Reciter
C = Chiden: Officer in Charge of the Ceremony Hall
D = Chiyoku: Bath Monk
E = Shika: Guestmaster
F = Chizō: Chief Librarian
G = Shoki: Clerical Officer
H = Tsūsu: Chief Supervisory Officer
I = Kansu: Supervisory Officer
J = Fūsu: Assistant Supervisory Officer in Charge of
      Revenue and Expenditures
K = Tenzo: Chief Cook
L = Shissui: Extern Sacristan
M = Shōko: Abbot's Incense Chaplain
N = Shōkyaku: Abbot's Guest-handling Chaplain
O = Shojō: Abbot's Secretarial Chaplain
P = Ehatsu: Abbot's Robe- and Bowl-handling Chaplain
Q = Tōyaku: Abbot's Food Chaplain
R = Jishō: Attendant on the Sacred Images in the Meditation
      Hall
S = Jishin: Sacristan
1 through 37 = other monks

MID-DAY SERVICE.

Sacristan: Have acolytes ring the meditation hall bells at 3:30 in the afternoon in the usual way.

Community: Either process to the ceremony hall, from the meditation hall, in the usual way or, if it is so desired or it is the time of the Searching of the Heart retreat for the community, sit in the meditation hall places in the usual way, facing outwards: Kesas should be worn: mats should be folded in front and placed under the edge of the Kesas.

Celebrant: Wear white under-robe, formal robe and Kesa and carry mat and lotus sceptre.

Celebrant's procession: Precentor, or assistant disciplinarian, with signal gong, celebrant and chaplain carrying one lighted stick of incense.

Celebrant: Process to the altar of the ceremony hall from the abbot's vestry in the usual way, or to the altar of the meditation hall from the abbot's vestry via the south door of the ceremony hall: proceed to the altar in the usual way and offer incense, both stick and powdered, in the usual way, make a wish for the peace of the community for the rest of the day and return to the bowing seat in the usual way.

Precentor: Do signal gong ring-down for the spreading of the celebrant's mat and then ring as usual for each of three bows.

> **Celebrant:** Make full, not seated, bows.
> **All:** Make three seated bows silently reciting one of the *Three Homages* with each bow.
> **Precentor:** Recite the following

Precentor

*R*ules for Meditation *

> **All:** Recite the following

All

Why are training and enlightenment differentiated since the Truth is universal? Why study the means of attaining it since the supreme teaching is free? Since Truth is seen to be clearly apart from that which is unclean, why cling to a means of cleansing it? Since Truth is not separate from training, training is unnecessary—the separation will be as that between heaven and earth if even the slightest gap exists * FOR, WHEN THE OPPOSITES ARISE, THE BUDDHA MIND IS LOST. However much you may be proud of your understanding, however much you may be enlightened, whatever your attainment of wisdom and supernatural power, your finding of the way to mind illumination, your power to touch heaven and to enter into enlightenment, when the opposites arise you have almost lost the way to salvation. Although the Buddha had great wisdom at birth, He sat in training for six years; although Bodhidharma Transmitted the Buddha Mind, we still hear the echoes of his nine years facing a wall. The Ancestors were very diligent and there is no reason why we people of the present day cannot understand. All you have to do is cease from erudition, withdraw within and reflect upon yourself. Should you be able to cast off body and mind naturally, the Buddha Mind will immediately manifest itself; if you want to find it quickly, you must start at once.

You should meditate in a quiet room, eat and drink moderately, cut all ties, give up everything, think of neither good nor evil, consider neither right nor wrong. Control mind function, will, consciousness, memory, perception and understanding; you must not strive thus to become Buddha. Cling to neither sitting nor lying down. When meditating, do not wear tight clothing. Rest the left hand in the palm of the right hand with the thumbs touching lightly; sit upright, leaning neither to left nor right, backwards nor forwards. The ears must be in line with the shoulders and the nose in line with the navel; the tongue must be held lightly against the back of the top teeth with the lips and teeth closed. Keep the eyes open, breathe in quickly, settle the body comfortably and breathe out sharply. Sway the body left and right then sit steadily, neither trying to think nor trying not to think; just sitting, with no deliberate thought, is the important aspect of serene reflection meditation.

This type of meditation is not something that is done in stages; it is simply the lawful gateway to carefree peace. To train and enlighten ourselves is to become thoroughly wise; the kōan appears naturally in daily life. If you become thus utterly free you will be as the water wherein the dragon dwells or as the mountain whereon the tiger roams. Understand clearly that the Truth appears naturally and then your mind will be free from doubts and vacillation. When you wish to arise from meditation, sway the body gently from side to side and arise quietly; the body must make no violent movement; I myself have seen that the ability to die whilst sitting and standing, which transcends both peasant and sage, is obtained through the power of serene reflection meditation. It is no more possible to understand natural activity with the judgmental mind than it is possible to understand the signs of enlightenment; nor is it possible to understand training and enlightenment by supernatural means; such understanding is outside the realm of speech and vision, such Truth is beyond personal opinions. Do not discuss the wise and the ignorant, there is only one thing—to train hard for this is true enlightenment; training and enlightenment are naturally undefiled; to live in this way is the same as to live an ordinary daily life. The Buddha Seal has been preserved by both the Buddhas in the present world and by those in the world of the Indian and Chinese Ancestors, they are thus always spreading the Truth—all activity is permeated with pure meditation—the means of training are thousandfold but pure meditation must be done. * It is futile to travel to other dusty countries thus forsaking your own seat; if your first step is false, you will immediately stumble. Already you are in possession of the vital attributes of a human being—do not waste time with this and that—you can possess the authority of Buddha. Of what use is it to merely enjoy this fleeting world? * This body is as transient as dew on the grass, life passes as swiftly as a flash of lightning, quickly the body passes away, in a moment life is gone. O sincere trainees, do not doubt the true dragon, do not spend so much time in rubbing only a part of the elephant; look

<u>inwards</u> and advance directly along the road that leads to the Mind, respect those who have reached the goal of goallessness, become one with the wisdom of the Buddhas, <u>Transmit</u> the wisdom of the Ancestors. ⁺ If you do these things for some time you will become as herein described and ⁺ then the Treasure House will open naturally and you will enjoy it fully.

Precentor: Recite the following offertory

Precentor

We offer the merits of this Scripture recitation to all so that they may be able to realize the Truth.

All: Recite the following

All

Homage to all the Buddhas in all worlds,
Homage to all the Bodhisattvas in all worlds,
Homage to *The Scripture of Great Wisdom.*

Precentor: Ring the signal gong for three bows.
Celebrant: Make three bows as before.
All: Make three bows as before, reciting one of the *Three Homages* with each bow silently.
Celebrant's recession: Precentor, or assistant disciplinarian, celebrant and chaplain return to abbot's vestry by the same route as that of the procession, leaving the meditation hall in the same way.
All: Rise from seats and stand in front of them with clasped hands.
Assistant disciplinarian: Ring the signal gong for the three gratitude bows.

All: Make three gratitude bows.

Community: Return to seats and sit down to remove Kesas, fold and place them with mats in Kesa cases: thereafter quickly and quietly leave the hall: if, however, the ceremony has been in the ceremony hall process back to the meditation hall and stand in front of seats for the three gratitude bows, thereafter removing Kesas, etc. as described in this paragraph. If there is meditation after mid-day service, gratitude bows are done at the end of meditation.

EVENING OFFICE.

Head novice: Strike the time block fifteen minutes prior to the time of evening meditation: ring the bells in the usual way.
All: No trainee may enter the meditation hall after the bells have finished ringing.
Precentor: At the end of meditation intone the following

Precentor

The Litany of the Great Compassionate One *

Musician: Play over the following

All: Chant the following

All

Adoration to the Triple | Treasure! :
  Adoration to Kanzeon Who is the Great
  Com|passionate One! ||
Om to the One Who leaps beyond all | fear! :

82

Having adored Him, — may I enter into the heart of the
    Noble, | Adored Kanzeon! ||
His life is the completion of | meaning; :
It is pure, — it is that which makes all beings
    victorious — and cleanses the | path of all
    existence. ||
Om, — O Thou Seer, — World-tran|scending One! :
O hail to the | Great Bodhisattva! ||
All, — all is defilement, defilement, earth, | earth. :
Do, do the | work within my heart. ||
O great Victor, I hold on, hold | on! :
To Indra the Cre|ator I cry! ||
Move, move, my defilement-|free One! :
Come, come, hear, hear, a | joy springs up in me! ||
Speak, speak, give me di|rection! :
Awakened, awakened, | I have awakened! ||
O merciful One, com|passionate One, :
Of daring ones the | most joyous, hail! ||
Thou art all suc|cessful, hail! :
Thou art the great suc|cessful One, hail! ||
Thou hast attained mastery in the | discipline, hail! :
Thou hast a weapon with|in Thine hand, hail! ||
Thou hast the Wheel within Thine | hand, hail! :
Thou Who | hast the lotus, hail! ||
Hail to Thee Who art the root of e|ternity! :
Hail to Thee Who | art all compassion! Hail! ||

Adoration to the Triple | Treasure! Hail! :

Give ear unto | this my prayer, hail! ||

Precentor: Precent the following and all other versicles as follows

Precentor

Invocation of Achala - na - tha *

Musician: Play over the following

Organ

Community: Chant the following and all other versicles

Community

Hail to the Mandala! — Let us so be engulfed within its praises evermore that, — by our own wills and vigilance, — may we our fetters | cut away. ||

May we within the temple of our own hearts dwell — amidst the myriad | mountains. ||

Hail! | Hail! Hail! ||

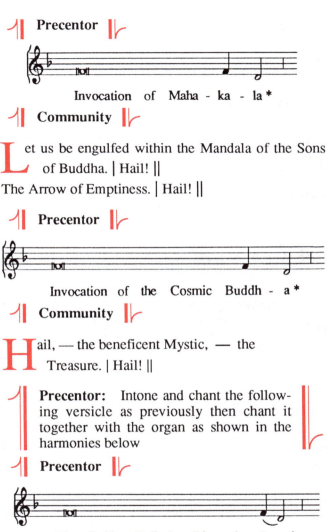

Precentor

Invocation of Maha - ka - la *

Community

L et us be engulfed within the Mandala of the Sons of Buddha. | Hail! ||

The Arrow of Emptiness. | Hail! ||

Precentor

Invocation of the Cosmic Buddh - a *

Community

H ail, — the beneficent Mystic, — the Treasure. | Hail! ||

Precentor: Intone and chant the following versicle as previously then chant it together with the organ as shown in the harmonies below

Precentor

The Golden Bell that Rings but Once *

Peace upon the | pillow. ||

◢❙ Organ and community ❙◣

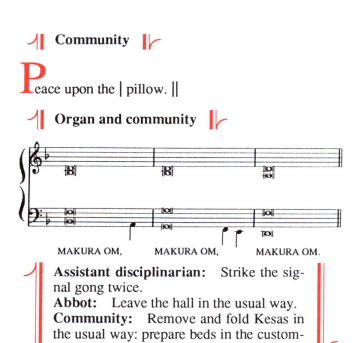

MAKURA OM,   MAKURA OM,   MAKURA OM.

Assistant disciplinarian: Strike the signal gong twice.

Abbot: Leave the hall in the usual way.

Community: Remove and fold Kesas in the usual way: prepare beds in the customary manner.

SCRIPTURAL RECITATION FOR SENDING BLESSINGS TO THE PRESIDENT AND PRAYERS FOR THE PEACE OF THE NATION.

Special note: The Scriptural Recitation for Sending Blessings to the President and Prayers for the Peace of the Nation is performed before morning service. In anticipation the sacristan places flowers and candles before the Buddha as well as arranges for sweet water, tea and cakes.

Community: Process into ceremony hall as for morning service. Spread mats fully, stand in usual places.

Abbot's procession: Abbot or representative, carrying fountain sceptre, goes to bowing seat and offers incense in usual way.

Assistant disciplinarian: Signal three bows after abbot returns to bowing seat.

Community: Pick up mats, face altar, spread mats fully, make three bows. After bows, pick up mats and turn to face each other as before; spread mats fully and stand on them.

Abbot, chaplains and acolytes: Move to positions for Great Monk's Offertory at first gong for abbot's incense offering. Chaplains and acolytes carry mats. At end of offertory, after putting pure paper and leaf in sleeve, abbot picks up fountain sceptre, all make monjin; chaplains and acolytes return to their starting positions, spread mats fully and stand on them; abbot returns to bowing seat.

Assistant disciplinarian: Signal three bows.

Abbot: Make three bows.

Precentor: Intone the following

Precentor

The Scripture of Great Wisdom

Community: Chant *The Scripture of Great Wisdom,* which is found on page 33.

Precentor: Chant the following offertory

Precentor

We look up to the lofty golden image, to the majestic Awakened Lord, to the Sole One revered throughout the three worlds and to all the myriad bright spirits. Every time the Temple meets at such an appointed hour, it respectfully gathers together the whole Sangha to recite with reverence *The Scripture of Great Wisdom* within the Treasured Hall of the Great Buddha. Out of deep gratitude and indebtedness we offer the merits thereof to the Great Benevolent Teacher, Great Master Shakyamuni Buddha, to the Highest Ancestor, Great Master Jōyō Dōgen, and to the Greatest Ancestor, Great Master Jōsai Keizan. Looking up to Them, we pray for Their great and vast benevolence and kindness; we bow down out of our awareness of Their perpetual wondrous virtue. Foremost we pray for the peace and tranquillity of the nation, for the long life of the president and for the peace and harmony of all sentient beings; may they realize the Highest Virtue with Its thousand joys.

Community: Face altar, make monjin at "Out of deep gratitude and indebtedness we offer the merits thereof to the Great Benevolent Teacher, Great Master Shakyamuni Buddha" and remain in monjin until "...perpetual wondrous virtue." At end of offertory chant *The Three Homages*.

Assistant disciplinarian: Signal three bows. At end of bows strike small gong twice for community to spread mats and sit on benches.

Community: Pick up mats, turn to face altar and spread mats fully, make three bows; spread mats on benches and sit.

Special note: Ceremony hall morning service, Founder's ceremony and trainees' spiritual examination ceremony follow. The ceremony then moves to the subsequent Recitation for the Guardian Deity.

SCRIPTURAL RECITATION FOR THE GUARDIAN DEITY.

Special note: When morning service is almost finished, the sacristy acolyte goes to the Guardian Deity's Shrine and places on it an incense box with lighted charcoal, tea and a candle. The community processes to the shrine after trainees' spiritual examination ceremony. The abbot or representative, carrying fountain sceptre, turns and faces south (altar). The chaplain offers the abbot the incense stick and the assistant chaplain the incense box. The abbot offers the incense stick, offers powdered incense, censes the tea in the smoke and offers it to the Guardian Deity.

Assistant disciplinarian: Signal three bows.

Special note: At abbot's discretion, bows are made either with full mat, Z-folded mat or standing.

Community: Make three bows as indicated by abbot.

Precentor: Intone the following

Precentor

The Litany of the Great Compassionate One

Community: Chant *The Litany of the Great Compassionate One*, which is found on page 39.

Precentor: Chant the following offertory

◢| **Precentor** |◣

Abundant and far-reaching are thy spiritual merits, clear and bright are Thy holy virtues; whenever we pray, we receive, without fail, a sympathetic response. We earnestly beseech Thee in Thy wisdom to shine Thy Light on us and protect us. Every time the community gathers at Thy shrine to recite *The Litany of the Great Compassionate One* we offer the merits therefrom to the great unfathomable Ocean of Virtue, that It may increase the benefic influence of this mountain's Guardian Deity, to the deity that protects this very place on the mountain and to all the good celestial beings and deities who defend the Dharma. We pray that this temple will be tranquil, that its trainees will be safe and secure, that our country will be at peace and that all nations will live in harmony with each other.

> **Community:**   Chant *The Three Homages.*
> **Assistant disciplinarian:** Signal three bows.
> **Community:**   Face north with abbot. Make three bows as before, followed by three gratitude bows facing altar.
> **Recession:**   Abbot and community recess to meditation hall for three final bows.

COMMEMORATIVE SERVICE
FOR THE ARAHANTS.

Special note: Performed in Arahant hall (or place where statues of Arahants are enshrined) in mid-morning. Arahant hall bell is rung in the usual way (if hall has no bell, use whatever bell is convenient). At Shasta Abbey this ceremony takes place in ceremony hall.

Community: Process to hall; chaplains, officers and rest of community take usual places.

Abbot or representative: Enter hall carrying fountain sceptre, offer incense in usual way.

Assistant disciplinarian: Signal three bows after abbot has returned to bowing seat.

Community: Spread mats fully, make three bows along with abbot. Pick up mats and turn to face monks across the hall; spread mats fully and stand on them.

Abbot, chaplains and acolytes: Move to positions at signal gong for Great Monk's Offertory. Chaplains and acolytes carry mats. At end of offertory, after putting pure paper and leaf in sleeve, abbot picks up fountain sceptre, all make monjin; chaplains and acolytes return to their starting positions and make three bows with rest of community.

Assistant disciplinarian: When abbot returns to bowing seat signal three bows.

Community: Pick up mats and face altar. Make three bows with abbot. After bows,

pick up mats, turn to face each other, spread mats fully and stand on them.
Precentor: Intone the following

Precentor

The Scripture of Great Wisdom

Community: Chant *The Scripture of Great Wisdom,* which is found on page 33.
Abbot: Make three offertory bows during chanting.
Precentor: Recite following offertory

Precentor

We offer the merits of this recitation of *The Scripture of Great Wisdom* to

Community: At this time chant the Holy Names of the Sixteen Arahants. There is one full bow after each name.
Assistant disciplinarian: Ring signal gong once for monks to chant each name and bow

Pindóla-bharadvája

Kánaka-vátsa

Kánaka-bharadvája

Supínda

Nákula

Bhádra

Kárika

Vajrapútra

Supáka

Pánthaka

Ráhula

Nagaséna

Íngata

Vanavási

Ájita

Chúda-pánthaka

Precentor: Continue with offertory

Precentor

...the Great Master Shakyamuni Buddha, the Highest Ancestor, Great Master Jōyō Dōgen and the Greatest Ancestor, Great Master Jōsai Keizan. We have offered flowers, fruit, candles, cakes and tea to the unsurpassed enlightenment of the Buddha. We pray that we may be able to show our gratitude to the Four Benefactors, assist all beings in the Three Worlds equally and make the Four Wisdoms perfect together with all living things.

Precentor: Continue with the following offertory

We offer the merits of this chanting of *The Scripture of Great Wisdom* to The Three Treasures in all the worlds.

Precentor: Lead abbot and community in *The Three Homages*.
Assistant disciplinarian: When abbot returns to bowing seat signal three bows.
Community: Pick up mats, face altar, spread mats fully, make three bows.
Abbot and community: At the end of bows make three gratitude bows and recess as usual.

OFFERING TO SHAKYAMUNI BUDDHA.

Sacristan: Prepare incense, flowers, candles, sweet water, cakes, tea and offerings for the main Buddha statue.

Procession: At 11:00 A.M., ring temple bell. Hall bell is then rung, monks process into ceremony hall and stand in usual places. Abbot or representative, carrying fountain sceptre, processes into hall, offers incense in usual way, returns to bowing seat.

Community: Make three full bows, pick up mats.

Abbot: Do not pick up mat; go to altar, offer incense, Great Monk's Offertory, monjin, return to bowing seat.

Offertory acolytes: Move to positions as usual. At the end of offertory make monjin with abbot, return to starting positions.

Assistant disciplinarian: Signal three bows.

Community: Make three full bows.

Precentor: At the end of the three bows intone *The Scripture of Great Wisdom*.

Precentor

*T*he Scripture of Great Wisdom

Community: Chant *The Scripture of Great Wisdom*, which is found on page 33.

Precentor: Intone following offertory

⫟ **Precentor** ⫙

We offer the merits of this recitation of *The Scripture of Great Wisdom* to the Great Master Shakyamuni Buddha, the Highest Ancestor, Great Master Jōyō Dōgen and the Greatest Ancestor, Great Master Jōsai Keizan. We have offered flowers, fruit, candles, cakes and tea to the unsurpassed enlightenment of the Buddha. We pray that we may be able to show our gratitude to the Four Benefactors, assist all beings in the Three Worlds equally and make the Four Wisdoms perfect together with all living things.

> **Community:** Chant *The Three Homages.*
> **Assistant Disciplinarian:** Signal three bows.
> **Community:** Make three bows followed by three gratitude bows.
> **Recession:** Abbot recesses as usual.
> **Special note:** Monks take their places for Shurangama ceremony which follows.

THE READING ALOUD OF
RULES OF THE TRAINEES' HALL.

Head of dormitories (Ryushu): After the noon meal prepare candles, incense box for statue in Shūryo (if no Shūryo, use meditation hall). Set out bowing seat, place copy of *Rules of the Trainees' Hall (Shūryo-shingi)* on lectern. If dining hall is large enough, this ceremony may be done there. Hang a sign outside the hall saying "Notice of Reading Aloud". (At Shasta Abbey this ceremony is done in meditation hall with community facing outwards and making seated bows as in mid-day service.)

Sacristan: Forty-five minutes after end of noon meal, strike time block in front of hall for full ring-down.

Community: Put on Kesas, carry copy of *Rules of the Trainees' Hall* wrapped in ceremonial cloth (fukusu), proceed to hall.

Recitation master: Offer incense and make monjin before statue.

Assistant disciplinarian: Ring signal gong.

Community: Make three full bows, sit in meditation.

Recitation master: Come forward, offer incense, return to place, sit in meditation position on mat, read *Rules of the Trainees' Hall* aloud.

Community: Listen silently with full attention.

*R*ules of the Trainees' Hall

The behaviour in the Trainees' Hall must be in accordance with the Precepts of the Buddhas and Ancestors as well as with the teachings of the Scriptures of the Hinayana and Mahayana, paying special attention to the rules of Hyakujō. Hyakujō states in his rules that our every action, whether great or small, must be in accordance with the Precepts of the Buddhas and Ancestors, therefore we must read the Vinaya and other Scriptures in the Trainees' Hall.

The Scriptures of the Mahayana and the words of the Ancestors must be read when in the hall; one must meditate deeply on the teachings of the old Zen Masters and try to follow those teachings.

Nyojō Zenji, my former master, once said to his trainees, "Have you ever read the Scripture delivered by the Buddha on His deathbed? Within this hall we must love each other and be deeply grateful for the opportunity of possessing a compassionate mind which enables us to be parents, relatives, teachers and wise priests; because of this compassionate mind our countenances will for ever show tenderness and our lives will for ever be blissful. We must never speak ill of another even if his language is coarse. We should speak tenderly to such a one, gently pointing out his fault, rather than defame him when he is not present. When we hear something of value we should put it into practice; by so doing we gain great merit. How fortunate it is that we are together. How fortunate it is that we, in this hall, have been able to make the acquaintance of those who, in former lives, performed good works and have thus become the treasures of the priesthood. What joy! Amongst the laity there is a great difference between related and unrelated persons, yet the Buddhist brotherhood possesses greater intimacy than most persons have with themselves. Zen Master Enan, of Ōryuzan, once said, 'the fact that we are in this boat is due entirely to our good deeds in past lives; that we are blessed with the opportunity of spending the training period together in the same monastery is equally due to the same cause. Although we are now in the position of master and trainees, one day we will all be Buddhas and Ancestors.' "

We must not disturb others by reading Scriptures or poetry in a loud voice when in the hall, nor may we hold a rosary when in others' presence. Herein all that we do must be gentle.

Visitors must never be permitted to enter the hall, nor may they be conversed with there, whatever their occupation. Those who must speak to shop-keepers must do so elsewhere.

Never talk idly or joke when in the hall. However great is the desire to laugh it must not be indulged in; we must always remember the four views of Buddhism:— there is impurity of body, pain in sensation, mind is transient and things have no ego; we must always remember to be devoted to Buddha, Dharma and Sangha. How can there be pleasure in a world wherein life is as transient as that of fish in a tiny pond? We must not chatter with fellow trainees; if we live an energetic life we can train our minds to become as mountains despite many others around us.

Never leave one's place to look at books which others may be reading: such behaviour is an obstacle both to one's own progress and to that of others in the study of Buddhism; than this, there is no greater misfortune.

If the rules of the Trainees' Hall are broken, and the offence is of a trifling nature, the guilty one must be duly warned by the seniors; if the offence is serious, the Disciplinarian must deal with the offender suitably after hearing the facts. Beginners, and those who have entered the priesthood late in life, must be warned compassionately and respectfully: as to whether or not they will obey this warning will depend upon the depth of sincerity in the mind of the individual trainee. The Temple Rules state that speech, deeds, and actions must be in accordance with the Trainees' Hall rules. Seniors must show an example to juniors, leading them as parents would lead their own children: this behaviour is in accordance with the mind of the Buddhas and Ancestors.

Worldly affairs, fame, gain, war, peace, the quality of offerings, etcetera, may never be discussed in the hall: such talk is neither significant nor useful, pure nor conscientious, and is strictly forbidden. It is to be understood that, since the Buddha has been dead for so long a time, our ability to gain enlightenment is too low to speak of. Time flies as an arrow and life is transient if we are slow in training. Wherever trainees may be from, they must make titanic efforts to train themselves just as they would, if their hair were to catch fire, make titanic efforts to extinguish the flames: time is precious and must never be wasted with idle chatter.

One must not pass in front of the holy statue in the hall, neither from the right nor left thereof, nor may one take notice of, or speak about, others' presence or absence; it is forbidden to look at others' seats.

One may not lie down, stretch the legs, lean against the woodwork or expose one's private parts when on one's seat for such behaviour is disturbing to others. The old Buddhas and Ancestors sat beneath trees, or in open places, and we should remember their very excellent behaviour.

Gold, silver, other money and clothes may not be hoarded in the hall: the old Buddhas made this clear in the Precepts. Makakashyo, the first Ancestor, when a layman, was a thousand times richer than King Bimbasara; in fact, his wealth was greater than that of all the sixteen countries of the time put together; however, once he left home and entered the priesthood, he wore ragged robes and had long hair, going begging until his death on Mount Kukkutapada: always the *funzoe* of the trainee comprised his clothes. One should understand very clearly that, since Makakashyo always appeared thus, we trainees of a later generation must be careful of our manners (if we are in the presence of those who are unkempt).

When speaking to another in the hall it must be in a quiet and polite voice. No noise must be made with slippers and noses may not be blown loudly; others must not be disturbed by spitting, coughing loudly, or yawning; one must learn the teaching of the Buddhas and Ancestors and not waste time with poetry. One may not read the Buddha's teachings loudly in the hall for this is rude to others.

If someone is impolite, he must be warned by the Disciplinarian; however important a senior is, he may not behave rudely or impolitely to others.

If one loses something, such as robes, bowls or anything else, the following notice must be exhibited on the board specially provided therefore:–

"Trainee.....lost.....on.....at..... I beg that whoever may find it shall exhibit a notice, similar to this, saying that it has been found." A great priest once said that, although one may be guilty in the sight of the law of the world and be punished, in the law of Buddhism one is beyond such punishment, therefore we must not make judgments or guesses of our own that may be detrimental to others' characters: the matter of dealing with lost articles must be in accordance with the rules of the temple. If a lost article is found by anyone, the fact must immediately be made public by a notice to the effect that it has been found.

Worldly, astrological or geographical books, heretical scriptures, philosophy, poetry or scrolls may not be left in the hall.

Bows and arrows, military equipment, swords, armour and other weapons are not permitted in the hall: if any person shall be in possession of a sword, he must be immediately expelled from the temple. No instruments for immoral purposes are permitted within the temple.

Musical instruments may not be played, nor dancing performed, in or near the hall.

Wine, meat, garlic, onions, scallions and horse-radish may not be brought into the hall.

When there are many in the hall, juniors must be quick to do laborious work; it is not, however, necessary for seniors to be so; this is traditional. Juniors must be slower than seniors in doing enjoyable work for this is the true law of the Buddhas.

All sewing must be done behind the hall: during this time, no idle chatter is allowed, for thoughts must for ever be upon the Buddhas and Ancestors.

Since the hall is for training only, no ill-mannered person is permitted to either enter or lodge there; those who are weak-minded, even if good-mannered, may not sleep therein or wander about for fear of disturbing others.

Worldly affairs and commerce may not be dealt with in the hall.

These rules are the Precepts of the Buddhas; in Eihei Temple [and Shasta Abbey] they must be observed for all time.

Precentor: Recite the following offertory

Precentor

We offer the merits of this reading of *Rules of the Trainees' Hall* to all so that they may be able to realize the Truth.

Community: Chant *The Three Homages.*

Assistant disciplinarian: Signal three bows.

Community: Make three bows followed by three gratitude bows.

Recitation master: Return to seat or leave hall.

Precentor: Strike small gong twice to signal end of ceremony.

Special note: When tea is served, recitation master and community take seats after three full bows. Tea master's acolyte (Chaju Anja) distributes tea cups then goes round pouring tea. When all have finished their tea, acolyte collects cups. When this is completed, community leaves after ring of signal gong for three gratitude bows.

MINDFUL RECITATION FOR THE CLOSING OF THE MEDITATION HALL.

Special note: This is performed on the day on which the meditation hall is closed so that the trainees may rest and bathe.
Community: Wear white under-robe, formal robe, Kesa, carry mat.
Two acolytes: Ring bell and beat wooden block alternately seven times standing in front of northern half of outside seats of meditation hall, see fig. 3.
Precentor: Recite the following

Precentor

The Light of Buddha is increasing in brilliance and the Wheel of the Dharma is always turning. These church buildings and this ground are guarding the Dharma and the trainees. All Meditations and Contemplations are full of treasure and wisdom and, because of them, we are going to pray to the Ten Buddhas.

All: Recite *The Names of the Ten Buddhas.*
Head novice: Strike meditation hall bell at beginning of each line.

All

The completely pure Buddha, Vairochana Buddha, Dharma Itself;

The complete Buddha Who has been rewarded for His previous training;

Shakyamuni Buddha, one of the many Buddhas Who has appeared in the many worlds;

Maitreya Buddha Who will appear in the future;

All the Buddhas in all directions and in the Three Worlds;

The great and excellent *Dharma Lotus Scripture;*

Holy Manjusri Bodhisattva;

The great and wise Samantabhadra Bodhisattva;

The great and kind Avalokiteshwara;

All the Bodhisattvas and Ancestors;

The Scripture of Great Wisdom.

> **Head novice:** Walk to centre of the meditation hall doorway, make monjin.
> **Head novice's assistant:** Walk behind head novice and a little to his left, carrying pole: give it to head novice when he asks.
> **Head novice:** Take pole from assistant: remove sign that says "Meditation Hall Open" and replace with sign that says "Meditation Hall Closed:" hand pole back to assistant, return to place.
> **Head novice's assistant:** Receive pole, return to place.
> **Head novice:** Recite following in firm, but quiet, voice

Head novice

Rest.

fig. 3

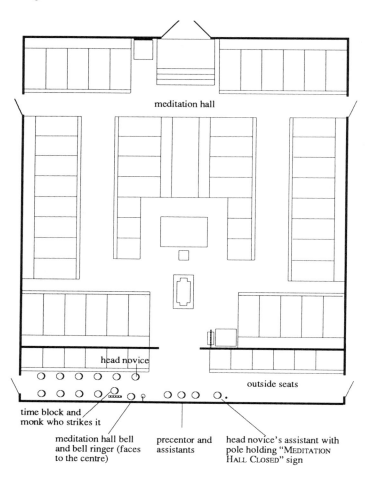

meditation hall

head novice

outside seats

time block and
monk who strikes it

meditation hall bell
and bell ringer (faces
to the centre)

precentor and
assistants

head novice's assistant with
pole holding "MEDITATION
HALL CLOSED" sign

O   monks

106

OPENING THE BATHS.

Bath Monk: Have monk responsible for the bath water (Suiju Anja) have his acolyte prepare for the opening of the baths which takes place after noon meal.

Acolyte: Before mid-day meal, set up a stand in bath house with a small, clean bucket on it, put stand in place for bathing Bodhisattva, provide flowers, incense stand, candles. Place clean towel on towel stand. (On clean towel there is sign reading "From the Director of the Baths, with Nine Bows". During term, Bathing of Bodhisattva is performed by head novice: sign should read "From the Head Novice, with Nine Bows".)

Bath Monk: After noon meal, bath monk hangs sign saying "Baths Open" outside bath house. Put on Kesa, strike drum three times. Proceed to bathe the Bodhisattva: enter meditation hall, make monjin before Manjusri, offer incense, return to bowing seat, make three full bows, invite Bodhisattva to bathe. Take clean bath towel from towel stand on return to bath house. Pour hot water into clean bucket, visualize Bodhisattva entering bath, spread mat, kneel upright on it, offer incense with left hand whilst holding towel in right hand. Cense towel in smoke, dip towel in tub, hold lightly in one hand, pour water from bucket on towel three times, recite the following once with each pouring

⌐| Bath monk ||⌐

As they cleanse their bodies, I pray that all sentient beings be beyond dirt in body and in mind and that their light shine pure and clean within and without.

Bath monk: Visualize eradication of Bodhisattva's form, offer incense, rise, make three bows, fold mat. Fold towel on stand, pour water from bathing Bodhisattva directly into bath for community to wash with. Go round corridors, hit each time block three times on way. Make single ring-down of seven strokes, ring-down and three strokes on bath drum (saku); at Shasta Abbey, great bell is used if bath drum is not available. Upon hearing this, abbot takes first bath, followed by temple officers from their dormitories (yakuryo). Ring down drum second time: those in meditation hall take baths: ring down drum third time. Monks in dormitories (ryoshu) take baths. Ring down "waning drum roll" (sakku); take own bath, monk in charge of water, servants and others take bath.

Community: When taking bath, having heard sequence of drum signals, put on small Kesa, take mat, enter bath house, face Sixteen Bodhisattvas (kaishi: 'They Who Open the Gate'). Usually there is only Bhadrapala Bodhisattva (Kengo Daishi), however the custom was originally to pray to the Sixteen Bodhisattvas in the bath house. Offer incense, spread mat, bow three times, recite the following

Community: Recites individually

As I cleanse my body, I pray that all sentient beings be beyond dirt in body and in mind and that our light shine pure and clean within and without.

In place for clothes, remove small Kesa, remove robe (jikitotsu), hang up with small Kesa on clothes horse. Turn to wall, remove underclothing, place on top of folded robes. Take bath towel, enter bathing area tranquilly. Stay outside bath tub, ladle hot water into small bucket, cleanse body thoroughly, remove all soap and soap skum, enter tub. Body must not be washed in tub; bodily dirt and grime may not be removed in tub. Do not thrash around in water, do not splash those nearby, do not hang legs over side of tub. Those who have ringworm, infected blisters from using moxa or use medications for skin diseases may not adhere to the bath drum sequence but must bathe last. Whilst in bath house, all conversation and singing are forbidden; maintain silence. If taps are not available in bath house, request adjustment of water temperature by striking small time block. Monk in charge of regulating water, upon hearing this, will adjust water. Voices may not be raised to call such monk. Board in front of small time block in bath house reads, "Strike once for hot water to be added. Strike twice for cold water to be added. Strike thrice to leave as is. Make moderations in this way." After bathing, wipe body dry, put on underclothes, put on robes, put on small Kesa, face Sixteen Bodhisattvas, spread mat, bow three times, return to dormitory.

Bath monk: If there is donor for opening of baths, such as one who has paid for fuel, affix donor's name below sign of "Baths Open" after having noted reason for donor's gift in Transfer of Merit before Sixteen Bodhisattvas.

Community: Similarly transfer merit when reciting scriptural invocation if it seems fitting. After bath, if donor has made offering of tea and cakes, monks partake of them in usual way, offering thanks to donor before returning to dormitory.

Bath monk: When bathing is completely over, together with monk in charge of bath water, extinguish furnace fires, carry unused firewood to its own place, see that all fires are extinguished. Put bath house equipment and implements back where they came from, sweep out interior of bath house.

Special note: On bath day there is no early morning meditation, mid-day service or Dharma talk after noon meal.

MEMORIAL FOR THE DEATH OF GREAT MASTER BODHIDHARMA.

Sacristy acolyte: Place bowing seat in front of Bodhidharma statue. Prepare altar with sweet water.

Sacristan: Prepare main altar in usual way.

Abbot and community: Enter hall in usual way and stand in usual places.

Abbot or representative: Carry fountain sceptre, go to front altar, offer incense, turn left, go to Bodhidharma Shrine, offer incense, make three full bows, offer sweet water, make monjin.

Assistant disciplinarian: Signal three bows as abbot returns.

Community and abbot: Make three bows.

Community: Pick up mats, stand in places.

Precentor: Intone *The Litany of the Great Compassionate One*

Precentor

*T*he Litany of the Great Compassionate One

Community: Chant *The Litany of the Great Compassionate One*, which is found on page 39.

Precentor: Intone the following offertory

111

◀| Precentor ||

The Dharma Body of the Buddha cannot be seen so long as one is within duality for It is beyond birth and death filling all things. Out of compassion for all living things the Buddha appeared in the form and figure of a human being; for this great act we bow in gratitude and pray that we may be able to illuminate our minds from delusion. We are gathered here today to commemorate the death of the First Ancestor, Engaku Daishi, Bodhidharma, and offer incense, flowers, candles and sweet water and the merits of the recitation of *The Litany of the Great Compassionate One* out of gratitude for his great compassion.

Community: Chant *The Three Homages.*
Assistant disciplinarian: Signal three bows.
Community: Make three bows, followed by three gratitude bows.
Special note: When mid-day service is omitted, the community processes directly out after making the three full bows and the three gratitude bows; they do not return to the meditation hall. (At Shasta Abbey community recesses to meditation hall to remove Kesas.)

SCRIPTURAL RECITATION FOR SKANDA.

Chief cook: When recitation of *Adoration of Buddha's Relics* has been reached during morning service, leave place and return to kitchen with kitchen acolyte who prepares flowers, candles, sweet water, cakes and tea before Skanda.

Kitchen acolyte: Hit Cloud Plate (umpan) in usual way.

Head novice: After morning service, lead community to kitchen and stand in two lines facing each other on right and left of altar.

Chief cook: Come out in front of kitchen to welcome abbot or representative.

Abbot: Offer incense at altar, make monjin, offer sweet water, cakes and tea. No bows.

Assistant disciplinarian: Strike signal gong three times.

Precentor: Intone *The Scripture of Great Wisdom*

Precentor

The Scripture of Great Wisdom

Community: Recite *The Scripture of Great Wisdom,* which is found on page 33.

Precentor: Intone *Invocation for the Removal of Disasters*

Precentor

Invocation for the Removal of Disasters

A – dor – – a – tion to all the Budd – has. A – dor –

a – tion to the lim – it – less teach – ing.

Peace! Speak! Blaze! Up! O-pen! To the glo-ri-ous, peace-ful

One for Whom there is no dis – – as – ter,

1. hail! Hail! A – dor –

2. Hail!

Precentor: Intone the following offertory

Precentor

We offer the merits of our recitation of *The Scripture of Great Wisdom* and the *Invocation for the Removal of Disasters* to Skanda, the Celestial Guardian of the Dharma enshrined here Who protects and guards the kitchen, that Divine Being Who oversees the fire and the hot water and Who protects the stoves. We earnestly pray that the temple will be tranquil, that those within and outside it be fully at peace, that fire and thieves pass it by and that benefactors and the faithful find refuge in and revere it.

> **Community**:   Chant *The Three Homages,* followed by three gratitude bows.
>
> **Abbot:**   Bow to chief cook, return to quarters.
>
> **Chief cook:**   Remain in front of kitchen, bow to abbot.
>
> **Meditation hall monks:**   Return to meditation hall.
>
> **Assistant disciplinarian:**   Come out of kitchen, ring signal gong twice (rōji shukei) as precentor leaves and those from various dormitories return to dormitories.
>
> **Kitchen acolyte:**   When assistant disciplinarian has finished ringing signal gong, strike Cloud Plate thirty-six times.

MONTHLY CELEBRATION FOR GREAT MASTER BODHIDHARMA.

Sacristy: Set up Bodhidharma altar with sweet water, cakes, tea and other food.

Special note: After mid-morning temple bell is rung, ceremony hall bell is rung and monks enter hall. Ceremony is the same as that for Bodhidharma anniversary on the previous day except that in the offertory text instead of "and sweet water" the phrase "sweet water, cakes, tea and other wondrous and savoury foods" is used. When this is over, monks move directly into midday service.

ABRIDGED FORM OF RENEWAL OF VOWS.

Sacristan: At 4:00 P.M. ring ceremony hall bell, after preparing incense, flowers and candles before Buddha statue, placing meditation chair in front of pillar on eastern (southern in Shasta Abbey) side of center (daima) of hall and placing small altar in front of chair with flowers, candle, holy water bowl, asperge and clappers upon it. A scroll can be hung with the names of the Buddhas upon it on a pillar.

Community: Process to hall.

Precentor: At third ring-down, process to vestry with assistant disciplinarian leading in front with signal gong, spread mat, bow three times, invite Precepts master to the ceremony.

Precepts master: Do not bow.

Precentor: Lead Precepts master into hall.

Assistant disciplinarian: Walk ahead of precentor and Precepts master, ring signal gong seven times.

Sacristan: Ring ceremony hall bell seven times, once after each of assistant disciplinarian's seven rings on signal gong.

Precepts master: Enter hall on seventh ring of bell.

Precentor: Keep distance of eight feet between self and Precepts master.

Chaplain: Follow behind Precepts master.

All the evil committed by me is caused by beginningless greed, hate and delusion.
All the evil is committed by our body, speech and mind;
I now confess everything wholeheartedly.

118

Homage to the Seven Buddhas of the Past,
Homage to Shakyamuni Buddha,
Homage to Maitreya, the Buddha Yet to Come,
Homage to Manjusri Bodhisattva,
Homage to Samantabhadra Bodhisattva,
Homage to Avalokiteshwara Bodhisattva,
Homage to the generations of Bodhisattvas who are the successive Ancestors and Masters of our Family.

> **Assistant disciplinarian:** Strike large gong once as precentor finishes reciting each name of Buddha. When precentor has finished reciting final line for last time, ring small gong once, then ring second time when community recites "the generations".
> **Community:** Stand on mats.
> **Assistant disciplinarian:** Strike small gong three times.
> **Precentor:** Gasshō, recite following Four Vows verse in loud voice

However innumerable beings may be, I vow to save them all,

However inexhaustible the passions may be, I vow to transform them all,

However limitless the Dharma may be, I vow to comprehend it completely,

However infinite the Buddha's Truth is, I vow to realize it.

> **Community:** Gasshō, repeat Four Vows verse in unison.
> **Precentor and community:** Repeat verse twice more, community repeating it after precentor has recited it.
> **Assistant disciplinarian:** Strike small gong as precentor finishes each Four Vows verse recitation; strike signal gong as community finishes each recitation.
> **Community:** Make one full bow after each ringing of signal gong.
> **Assistant disciplinarian:** When both precentor and community have finished third recitation, strike signal gong twice.

> **Community:** Make third bow, rise, stand on mats.
> **Assistant disciplinarian:** Signal three bows for Precepts master.
> **Precepts master:** Go to main altar, offer incense, make three bows, sit on meditation chair.

Precentor

With three bows we invite the Precepts master to speak.

> **Assistant disciplinarian:** Signal three bows.
> **Community:** Make three bows, place mats on benches and sit.
> **Precepts master:** Take holy water from head, bless water in asperge bowl.
> **Precentor:** Stand in front of Precepts master.
> **Precepts master:** Give asperge bowl to precentor.
> **Precentor:** Asperge community, return asperge bowl to Precepts master.
> **Precepts master:** Gasshō, strike clappers three times, once at beginning of each of three recitations of following lecture verse

Precepts master

The unsurpassed, penetrating and perfect Truth
Is seldom met with even in a hundred, thousand myriad kalpas.
Now we can see and hear it, we can remember and accept it;
I vow to make the Buddha's Truth one with myself.

Assistant disciplinarian: At end of third recitation of lecture verse, strike signal gong once for precepts master to begin recitation of the Introduction for the Reading from *The Scripture of Brahma's Net.*

Precepts master: Recite or chant the following Introduction for the Reading from *The Scripture of Brahma's Net,* then *The Scripture of Brahma's Net* itself.

Community: Gasshō, give selves over completely to listening, remain in gasshō until Scripture is finished.

Precepts master

Disciples of the Buddha, with your hands in gasshō, listen with the utmost attention. Listen to the Great Precepts of the Buddhas. O assembly of monks, hearken to me in utter silence. You should do sange knowing that you have defiled yourselves for, when there is sange, there is peacefulness and contentment; the increase in defilement is profound without sange. Let those who are without defilements remain silent; those of you who are silent have realized the immaculacy of the monastic assembly. Likewise listen carefully, you laity of both genders who are of great virtue. After the Buddha's parinirvana, during the period when the Teaching will be treated superficially, honour and respect the Pratimokshas which are the practices that lead to liberation; the Pratimokshas are none other than these Precepts. When you keep to the Precepts it is as darkness meeting light, as a poor man receiving a treasure, as a sick person regaining his balance, as a chained prisoner being released from jail, as a traveller to distant lands returning home; you should know that these Principles are the Great Teachers of this assembly. When a Buddha abides in the world They are the same for Him as for us. A reverent heart is difficult to beget, a good heart is difficult to give rise to; this is why the Scripture says, 'Do not treat small defilements lightly or regard them to be harmless.' Even though drops of water are minute, they gradually fill a large container; it takes but a moment to produce a defilement whose calamities will fall down upon you incessantly. Once you have lost your human body you may not regain one for ten thousand kalpas; a robust physique does not last for it is as a runaway horse. Human life is impermanent, it flows away as does water down a mountain; although you exist to-day, tomorrow is hard to guarantee. Each of you in this assembly must be wholehearted in your devotion to diligent training. Be careful not to give in to laziness, negligence, idleness, drowsiness or thoughts of self-indulgence. At night, as you concentrate your mind, keep the Three Treasures in your thoughts. Do not beget deep regrets in later generations because of fatigue brought on by your vacuity, errors and vanity. Let each of you here assembled be wholehearted in your endeavours to live according to these Precepts; train and study in accordance with the Teachings.

Precentor (or head novice during term time): Recite the following in loud voice

The universe is as the boundless sky,
  As lotus blossoms above unclean water;
Pure and beyond the world is the Buddha Nature of the
    trainee;
O Holy Buddha, we take refuge in Thee.

> **Precepts master:** Leave meditation chair.
> **Assistant disciplinarian:** Strike signal gong twice.
> **Community:** Rise, spread mats fully.
> **Assistant disciplinarian:** Strike large gong thrice.
> **Precentor:** Gasshō, chant text of *The Three Refuges*. Draw out voice during intonation.

Precentor

I take refuge in the Buddha, wishing all sentient beings to understand the great doctrine and make the superlative resolution for Buddhahood.

I take refuge in the Dharma, wishing that all sentient beings shall penetrate the great Scriptures with wisdom as unfathomable as the ocean.

I take refuge in the Sangha, wishing that all sentient beings shall be able to live in harmony, as well as harmonize the general multitudes, without any obstructions whatsoever and that all shall respect the sacred Sangha.

> **Community:** Gasshō. After the words "I take refuge in the Buddha", join in recitation with precentor. Make one full bow at end of each refuge.
> **Assistant disciplinarian:** When words "I take refuge in the Buddha" have been recited, strike large gong once; ring signal gong at end of each refuge once; when words "I take refuge in the Dharma" have been recited, strike large gong once; when words "I take refuge in the Sangha" have been recited, strike large gong once again.

Sacristy acolyte: Remove lectern at end of phrase "sentient beings".

Precepts master: Recite or chant following offertory

Precepts master

We offer the merits of this reading of the Precepts to all in the Dharma World out of reverence for all the disciples of the Buddha.

Community: Chant *The Three Homages*.

Assistant disciplinarian: Signal three bows.

Community: Make three bows.

Abbot and community: At end of bows make three gratitude bows and recess as usual.

Special note: Since the reading of the Precepts is essential to the Renewal of Vows, the reading of the Precepts should be done even though, at the Precepts master's discretion, it may be deleted for simplicity's sake; when circumstances require their deletion, once the Four Vows have been recited, *The Three Refuges* are immediately recited and, instead of the line "The merits of this reading of the Precepts" in the offertory, the line "The merits of this renewal of our Vows" is substituted. In the month of December the Renewal of Vows is done one day earlier, that is, on the thirtieth. With the ordinary Renewal of Vows there are occasions when the reciting of *The Scripture of Brahma's Net* is abridged, but see that the reading of *The Scripture of Brahma's Net* is not completely omitted.

EVENING SPIRITUAL EXAMINATION AND SERVING OF TEA.

Tea monk's acolyte (Chaju Anja): Prepare for serving of tea in tea hall, abbot's guest room or in ceremony hall. At Shasta Abbey this ceremony is done in dining hall. Set up incense stand with incense box in centre of room, put small quantity of tea cakes in tea bowl and arrange two trays for serving tea. Set out low table and serving tray with plate of tea cakes for abbot, prepare Bancha tea in large earthen pot or in tea kettle, put on stand in front of tea monk's place. Bancha is evening tea. Ring evening bell, strike tea drum one full ring-down. (At Shasta Abbey ring great bell one full ring-down if no tea drum).

Community: Wear small Kesa, process to tea hall.

Chaplain: Process with abbot to tea hall from abbot's quarters.

Abbot or representative: Enter tea hall.

Community: Bow together with abbot when he enters, all sit.

Chaplain: Offer tea to abbot.

Tea monk's acolyte: Distribute tea cups to community.

Tea monk's second acolyte: Go round pouring tea.

Community: When all have been served, partake of tea together.

Tea monk's first and second acolytes: Serve tea a second time. When all tea is finished, collect utensils.

Abbot: It is customary at such a tea to make an offering of tea and cakes. It is also customary to make remarks, if there are any to be made, on the Precepts, such as matters to which to pay particular attention.

Community: Listen to abbot's remarks respectfully, with heads lowered.

Assistant disciplinarian: Ring down large work drum (meiku).

Community: All bow together, process from hall.

Special note: If western hall or an administrative officer has instructions for community, he waits until the drum has been struck and the abbot has returned to his quarters. Community resume seats to listen to his comments.

Western hall or administrative officer: Make comments.

Assistant disciplinarian: Ring signal gong twice.

Community: Rise from seats and leave hall in usual way.

Administrative and other officers: Go together to abbot's quarters to arrange for following morning's ceremony.

MEMORIAL SERVICE FOR THE DEATHS OF THE TWO ANCESTORS DŌGEN AND KEIZAN.

Special note: "Ancestors' Shrine and statues" in Shasta Abbey refers to Founder's Shrine (Kōhō Zenji Shrine). All of this ceremony would take place within Founder's Shrine itself if that shrine were large enough.

Founder's Shrine monk: Prepare incense, flowers, candles before statues, ikons or pictures of two Ancestors, prepare sweet water.

Founder's Shrine acolyte: When closing ceremony for meditation hall is finished and bell announcing closure has been rung slowly three times, ring bell in ceremony hall one full ring-down.

Head novice: Lead community directly from closing ceremony to ceremony hall.

Community: Take places as usual.

Abbot or representative: Carrying fountain sceptre, process into ceremony hall, make monjin on bowing seat; walk to Founder's Shrine, go to statues, ikons or pictures, offer incense, return to bowing seat in ceremony hall, make three full bows.

Assistant disciplinarian: Signal three bows.

Community: Make three full bows with abbot, pick up mats, stand.

Abbot: Spread mat fully, go to altar in Founder's Shrine, offer sweet water, return to bowing seat in ceremony hall, make three bows alone, pick up mat, stand.

Assistant discipinarian: Strike signal gong three times.

Precentor: Intone *The Scripture of Avalokiteshwara Bodhisattva*

Precentor

The Scripture of Avalokiteshwara Bodhisattva.

Community: Chant *The Scripture of Avalokiteshwara Bodhisattva*, which is found on page 2; circumambulate whilst doing so. Head novice leads circumambulation on north side to Founder's Shrine; monks offer incense at incense boxes provided, then continue to south side, circumambulating as usual. Monks on south side circumambulate as usual, connecting with back row on north side, follow to Founder's Shrine, offer incense and continue circumambulation to starting position.

Precentor: Chant following offertory

Precentor

From Great Compassion comes forth the Pure Dharma Body, unborn, uncreated. We pray that the darkness of our delusion may be illuminated by True Compassion. Whenever the Temple meets at this appointed time, we devotedly prepare incense, flowers, candles and sweet water, and we humbly gather the Sangha together to recite with reverence *The Scripture of Avalokiteshwara Bodhisattva*. We offer the merits of our gathering here to the Highest Ancestor, Great Master Jōyō Dōgen, and to the Greatest Ancestor, Great Master Jōsai Keizan, in recompense for their benevolence and kindness. We humbly pray that they will not abandon their compassionate hearts but take pity on those in the six realms of existence in all three worlds, that they will return in these last degenerate days of the Law to reveal the springtime of the Single Blossom with Its five leaves and that they will protect the disciples of later generations and perpetuate our Ancestral tradition for ages yet to come.

> **Community:** Chant *The Three Homages.*
> **Assistant disciplinarian:** Signal three bows.
> **Community:** Make three full bows, followed by three gratitude bows, recess.

MONTHLY CELEBRATION FOR THE TWO ANCESTORS DŌGEN AND KEIZAN.

Special note: All of this ceremony would take place within Founder's Shrine itself if that shrine were large enough.

Founder's Shrine monk: After mid-day meal bell has been rung, ring bell in ceremony hall one full ring-down.

Community: Enter ceremony hall, take usual places.

Abbot or representative: Celebrate using same sequence of actions as was done the night before for memorial ceremony; instead of the usual offerings however, offer sweet water, cakes, tea and fragrant rice.

Precentor: Intone *The Scripture on the Immeasurable Life of the Tathagata*

Precentor

*T*he Scripture on the Immeasurable Life of the Tathagata *

Musician: Play over the following

Community: Chant *The Scripture on the Immeasurable Life of the Tathagata*;

circumambulate as done during memorial ceremony.

Community

The World-|honoured One, | then desiring to reiterate the Teaching's meaning, | spoke | thus in verse: :

"Since I have realized Buddhahood, | the aeons through which I have passed are immeasurable hundreds of thousands of | millions of billions. ||

Contin|uously have I voiced the Dharma, | teaching untold billions of beings how to turn their hearts around that they might enter the | Buddha's path; :

To ferry these sentient beings to the Other Shore I reveal to them, | by skilful means, | My parinirvana yet truly I am not extinct but always abiding here | giving | voice to the Dharma. ||

* I con|tinue to abide in this world, | using my spiritual powers to make confused creatures not see Me, | though I am near, | so that they may look on Me as extinct and make offerings | to My relics, :

Cherishing longing desires | and giving rise to hearts | thirsting for hope. ||

When these | sentient beings in faith and humility, | honest and forthright in manner, | gentle in thought, | wholeheartedly yearn to see the Buddha, | not begrudging even | their own lives, :

132

Then I, with all the Sangha, appear together on the Di|vine Vulture Peak. ||

I then | tell these sentient beings that I continue to abide here with|out extinction; :

By the power of my skilful methods I show myself as extinct, | even though not extinct. ||

If in some | other region there are beings reverent and with | faith beseeching, :

Again I am in their midst to proclaim the unsurpassed Dharma, ¹ though you who do not hear this will | say that I am extinct. ||

When I | behold sentient beings sunk in their suffering | and distress, :

I do not show myself but set them all to look up in their thirsting and, ¹ when their hearts are filled with fervent longing, ¹ I then appear and pro|claim the Dharma. ||

Such are my | spiritually pervading powers that, ¹ through-out the boundless aeons, ¹ I abide on the Di|vine Vulture Peak :

As well as in every | other dwelling place. ||

When sen|tient beings see, ¹ at kalpa's ending, ¹ the raging fires con|suming all, :

Tranquil will this realm of Mine be, ¹ ever filled with devas and humans in parks and groves, ¹ amongst towers and palaces bedecked with | gems of every kind. ||

Under be|jewelled trees, ǀ heavy with blossoms and fruit,ǀ may these beings take their de|light and play, :

Whilst devas beat their heavenly drums, ǀ ever making pleasing music, ǀ and showering down coral tree flowers upon the Buddha and | His great assembly. ||

My Pure | Land will not be destroyed, ǀ though sentient beings may see it as utterly con|sumed by fire, :

Letting themselves be filled with grief and horror, ǀ | distress and fear. ||

All these | besmirched creatures pass through countless aeons, ǀ hearing not the name | of the Triple Treasure :

Due to | their wretched karma. ||

Those who | practise deeds of merit and are gentle, hon|est and forthright, :

All see Me in body and hear Me | voice the Dharma. ||

At times | for the sake of that assembly I tell them that a Buddha's | life is immeasurable, :

Then to those who, ǀ at long last, ǀ see a Buddha I say that a | Buddha is rarely met. ||

Such is the | power of My wisdom and intelligence that My light of insight shines forth | beyond measure, :

My life of countless aeons is due to the karma of long | practice and training. ||

* You who | have intelligence and wit, ǀ do not let doubts arise in | this regard, :

But sever them from yourself and bring them forever to an end ⏐ for the Buddha's Words are true, ⏐ not something that is | empty and vain. ||

Just as the | physician who would cure his demented sons by clever and skilful methods ⏐ proclaims his own death whilst, in fact, he is alive, ⏐ and none can say he | willfully lies, :

I, too, ⏐ being as a parent to this world, ⏐ as one who helps all those in misery and affliction ⏐ because of the topsy-turvy views of these ordinary people, ⏐ say I am extinct, though | I am truly alive. ||

I do | this lest, by always seeing Me, they should beget hearts unrestrained and | self-indulgent, :

Be dissolute and only fixed upon the five forms of desire ⏐ and thereby | fall into evil ways. ||

* I know | at all times whether a sentient being is treading the Path or | walks in other ways :

And, ⏐ according to what needs to be done to aid that one, ⏐ voice Teachings of various kinds, ⏐ making for each | this my intention, ||

'How may | I help this being enter the | unsurpassed Way :

And quickly | realize Buddhahood?'" ||

Precentor: Recite same offertory as that used for memorial service on previous day except that, instead of "and sweet water", say "sweet water, cakes, tea and other wondrous and savoury foods", also substitute name of Scripture recited for this ceremony.

Community: Chant *The Three Homages.*

Assistant disciplinarian: Signal three bows.

Community: Make three full bows, followed by three gratitude bows, recess.

Special note: Mid-day services are omitted on this day.

Kitchen acolyte: Strike cloud plate thirty-six times.

Special note: Formal noon meal follows.

MONTHLY CELEBRATION FOR
THE FOUNDER OF ONE'S TEMPLE.

Special note: This ceremony is identical with that of the Monthly Celebration for the Two Ancestors on the twenty-eighth and twenty-ninth days. With a restored temple the ceremony should be patterned after this one with suitable alterations. The precentor chants or recites the following offertory

Precentor

From Great Compassion comes forth the Pure Dharma Body, unborn, uncreated. We pray that the darkness of our delusion may be illuminated by True Compassion. On this ... day of ... we reverently meet to commemorate the death of Great Master ..., Founder of the monastery and, in devotion, have prepared incense, flowers, candles, sweet water, cakes, tea and other wondrous and savoury foods. In addition we offer him/her the merits of the Sanghas respectfully gathering here to recite ... in recompense for his/her benevolence and kindness. We humbly pray that he/she will not abandon his/her compassionate heart but take pity on those in the six realms of existence in all three worlds, that he/she will return during these last degenerate days of the Law to reveal the springtime of the Single Blossom with Its five leaves and that he/she will protect the disciples of later generations and assist our Ancestral tradition for ages yet to come.

Special note: The following is an abridged form of offertory which can be recited by the precentor.

◢ **Precentor** ▐▟

We pray that the darkness of our delusion may be illuminated by True Compassion. We respectfully offer the merits of our gathering here to recite ... to Great Master ..., Founder of this monastery, in recompense for his/her benevolence and kindness.

> **Special note**: Upon reaching the phrase "of Great Master ..., Founder of this monastery" the community, in adoration, turns towards the altar, makes monjin and remains in monjin until "...benevolence and kindness."

MONTHLY CELEBRATION FOR A VENERABLE ELDER OR PREVIOUS ABBOT.

Special note: On the memorial anniversary of a previous abbot of the temple or on the memorial anniversary of a venerable elder renowned for his or her meritorious deeds, services are performed with an offering of sweet water on the eve and sweet water, cakes, tea and fragrant rice at the memorial ceremony on the following day. The following offertory is recited by the precentor on the eve.

Precentor

Jewel bright is the Boundless Sea, its surface churning with the waves of births and deaths; the gate to the Great Tranquillity dissolves the shapes of past and present, the forms of coming and going. We pray that the darkness of our delusion may be illuminated by True Compassion.

THE FESTIVAL OF THE BIRTH OF THE HIGHEST ANCESTOR DŌGEN.

Special note: This is identical with the Festival Memorial for Great Master Eihei Dōgen, to be found on page 337 of the Priests' Book, with the exception that the Scripture recited is *The Scripture on the Conduct that Eases the Way* and that a different offertory is chanted or recited by the precentor (see below).
Precentor: Intone the following

The Scripture on the Conduct that Eases the Way

Community: Chant or recite

The World-honoured One, desiring to clarify the meaning of His Teaching, spoke thus in verse:

"If there be any Bodhisattva here who, in the evil days to come, with a heart free from fear and awe, desires to preach on this Discourse of Mine, you must hold to a Bodhisattva's perspectives on practice and relationships.

Be constant in keeping your distance from those who would rule and their offspring, ministers and officials, from those who play at brutal and dangerous games, are devoid of scruples or steer their lives by chance as well as from non-Buddhists such as Brahman priests.

Seek no friendship or companionship among those vain and conceited ones who avidly pursue the Lesser Course in their study of the Triple Canon, with

140

Precept-breaking monks who are Arahants in name only, with monks who take joy in flirtatious laughter, with those who are deeply attached to all manner of craving or are seeking instant nirvana, as is common with lay folk; with none of these seek familiarity.

However, if such people, out of goodness of heart, come to you as a Bodhisattva to hear of the Buddha's Way, then, as a Bodhisattva with heart free from fear and awe and cherishing no expectations, you should speak with them on the Teaching.

Do not seek to entice into intimacy or close friendship such as are widowed, young or equally vulnerable to some form of seduction; do not keep company with butchers, meat-cutters, hunters or fishermen, for they slaughter and slay for gain; do not keep company with those who hawk meat for their living and those who parade and market people for sex; do not consort with such ones.

With violent and dangerous sports and all manner of frivolous games, as well as with dissolute people, you should not seek to involve yourself whatsoever.

You should not, in some screened-off place, talk about the Teaching alone with one of the opposite sex.

When you preach on the Dharma, take care to avoid making a joke of it.

When entering a village in quest of food, seek a monk to accompany you; if no monk is available, keep your mind wholeheartedly on the Buddha.

These, then, are what are called the perspectives on practice and relationships.

By maintaining these two perspectives you can teach with ease and contentment.

Further, when you do not act as if there were superior, middling and inferior Dharmas, or as though things were material or independent of cause, real or unreal, when you do not make such distinctions as 'This is a man' or 'This is a woman', and when you do not grasp after things, failing to recognize them because you do not discern them as desirable, this then is what is called a Bodhisattva's perspective on practice.

All that are called 'things' are void of self-existence, having no permanence, neither arising nor perishing: this is what wise ones call a Bodhisattva's perspective on relationships, whereas those whose views are topsy-turvy decide by discrimination whether all things exist or do not exist, are real or unreal, produced or not produced.

As for you, abide in seclusion, train and pacify your mind, dwelling peaceably in your meditation and immovable as Mount Sumeru, regarding all things as though they had no permanence, as if they were as insubstantial as space, lacking solidity, not arising or coming forth but motionless and unreceding, ever remaining in their oneness: this is what is called a Bodhisattva's perspective on relationships.

If there be any monk who, after My entering into eternal meditation, holds to these perspectives on practice and relationships, then, when he talks on this Discourse of Mine, he will have no timidity or weakness.

When this Bodhisattva at times enters the quiet of his room and, whilst holding properly to mindfulness, looks upon all things according to their true significance, let him then rise from his meditation and, for the sake of rulers of nations, their offspring and subjects, be they Brahmans and others, help turn their hearts around by clearly expounding and explaining this Discourse of Mine with a heart and mind at ease, free from timidity and weakness.

O Manjusri, this is what is called a Bodhisattva's being steadfast in the first means for he will then be able, in future generations, to preach on this Discourse which is the blossoming of My Teaching.

"A Bodhisattva ever delights, and is at ease, in giving voice to the Dharma; in a pure and clean place he spreads out his mat, anoints himself with sesame oil after having bathed away dust and dirt, puts on a fresh, clean robe so that he is completely clean within and without and then, calmly seated on his Dharma seat, he teaches according to how he is questioned.

Be there monks of either gender, lay disciples of either gender, rulers, their offspring, and retainers or other people, he expounds the subtlest meanings to them all, ever with a gentle countenance.

If there is any objection or difficult question, he responds to it according to its meaning, elaborating and making distinctions through apt illustrations and parables.

By these skilful means he urges them all to give rise to their will to train so that, steadily advancing, they may penetrate the Buddha's Way.

Having rid himself of any tendencies to indolence and of any idle thoughts and fancies, he is free from all worry, grief and care and, with a tender and compassionate heart, proclaims the Dharma, day and night, ever propounding the unsurpassed Teaching of the Way by varied illustrations and innumerable parables, he reveals It to sentient beings which causes them all to rejoice.

Of garments, bedding, drink, food, medicine and all such things he has no expectations; with singleness of mind, he thinks only of the cause of his teaching the Dharma, vowing to complete the Buddha's Path by helping all others to do the same; this is his great reward, contentment and offering.

After My entering into eternal meditation, if there be any monk capable of proclaiming this Discourse which is the wondrous blossoming of My Teaching, his heart will be free from envy and rancour, from all irritations and obstacles, and from sorrow and depression as well as from the curses and slanders of others.

Further, he will be free from fear and dread of their adding the insult of injury from sword or cudgel; he will not be driven off for he is steadfast and at ease in his forbearance.

The wise one, in such ways as these, will train his mind so well, and be able to dwell so content and at ease, as I have already said, that the merits and virtues of this person are beyond any power to fully express in number or in illustration even were thousands upon thousands of kalpas to be given for the task.

If you wish to give voice to this Discourse of Mine, you
should forsake all envy, anger and pride and all
thoughts arising from a suspicious, deceitful, twisted
or dishonest heart, ever cultivating the practice of
maintaining integrity.

Do not disparage others or, for amusement's sake,
discuss the Teachings or lead others to doubt or
regret by saying: 'You will never become Buddhas'
but, as a disciple of the Buddha, when giving voice
to the Dharma, be ever gentle, patient and compassionate with all, never cultivating thoughts of
indulgence or idleness.

Toward the great Bodhisattvas in all the Ten Quarters
who practice the Way out of pity for all beings
cultivate a reverent mind by thinking, 'These
are my great teachers'; for all World-honoured
Buddhas engender thoughts of them as peerless
parents and then, eliminating all feelings of pride
and arrogance, give unobstructed voice to the
Dharma.

Such is the third method: let the wise protect and guard
it for wholehearted devotion to these practices in
ease and contentment is revered by beings beyond
count.

Ever act with patience and forbearance, and with pity
for all beings, for only then can you give voice to a
Discourse which the Buddhas will extol.

In later ages to come, you who would keep to this
Discourse of Mine, be you layman, monk or one not
yet on the Bodhisattva path, by all means cultivate
compassion by thinking, 'Since those who do not
hear, or have faith in this Discourse of His, will

suffer a great loss, I, having realized the Buddha Way through skilful means, will expound this Dharma to them that they all may abide in It.'

Like a powerful monarch whose chariot wheels roll everywhere, one who, to his soldiers who are meritorious in battle, presents many rewards such as elephants, horses, chariots, carriages and ornaments to adorn their bodies, as well as fields, houses, villages and cities, or gives them raiment, various kinds of precious jewels, servants and wealth, joyfully bestowing all, but only for the one who is most valiant and strong and capable of the most difficult of deeds does the monarch take from his own head the lustrous pearl to give to him, so too is it with a Tathagata; Lord of all Dharmas, Whose great strength lies in His patience and His treasure Trove of enlightened wisdom.

Out of His great compassion and benevolence, and in keeping with the Dharma, He transforms the world.

Seeing all human beings suffering in torment and distress, and craving to find deliverance as they struggle against the demons of Mara, He gives voice to various Teachings for the sake of all these sentient beings and, by the most skilful of means, proclaims the various Scriptures but, once He finally knows for sure that these beings have their full strength, then, and only then, at last, does He offer this Flower of the Dharma to them just as the monarch took from his head the bright pearl as his gift.

This Discourse of Mine is the most precious among all the Scriptures; I have always guarded It, kept It safe and never revealed It rashly or too soon; now, indeed, this is the time to proclaim It to you all.

After My entering into eternal meditation, whoever seeks the Buddha's Way and desires peaceably and amicably to give voice to this Discourse of Mine should make himself intimate with the four modes of conduct as they have been given.

Whoever of you reads this Discourse completely, and attends to Its meaning, will be ever free from worry, grief, gloom, suffering and disease, of countenance bright and clear; you will not live in destitution, meanness or squalor and all sentient beings will delight to look upon you with a fondness they feel for one sainted or wise; the offspring of devas will be given you as ministers; swords and cudgels will not add their injury to you; things poisonous will leave you unharmed.

If any, from hatred or malice, would abuse you, their mouths will close up tight; fearless will you roam like the Lord of lions and the radiance of Your wisdom and insight will shine forth illumining like the sun.

When you dream, you will behold only things wondrous; you will see Tathagatas, seated upon their Lion Thrones of Meditation, as They give voice to the Dharma to the hosts of surrounding monks: you will behold nagas and spirits, asuras and others, in number as the sands of the Ganges, as they pay reverence with hands held in gasshō, and you will catch sight of yourself proclaiming the Dharma to them.

You will also behold Buddhas, Their bodies like
burnished gold, emitting boundless rays of light
which illumine all as, with voices melodious as
Brahma's, They thunder forth the Dharma.

Whilst some Buddha gives voice to the Supreme Dharma
to the fourfold host of disciples, you will see yourself in their midst extolling the Buddha with your
hands in gasshō.

On hearing the Dharma, you will fill with joy and,
making your offering, will receive the sacred invo-
cations and give witness to the wisdom of never
regressing.

The Buddha, knowing that, in heart and mind, you have
penetrated deep into the Buddha's Way, will then
predict your success in realizing Supreme and
Perfect Enlightenment, saying, 'You, my good child,
shall, in an age to come, obtain wisdom beyond
measure by realizing the Great Way of the Buddha.

Your realm will be splendrous and immaculate, of
breadth beyond compare; there you too will have
your fourfold host of disciples who, with hands in
gasshō, will listen to you proclaim the Dharma.'

You will also see yourself in some mountain grove
putting the good Teachings into practice by proving
for yourself what is real and what appearance and,
deep in meditation, you will meet the Buddhas of all
the Ten Quarters.

Like burnished gold are the bodies of these Buddhas,
adorned with a hundred auspicious marks, for
whoever, hearing the Dharma, gives voice to It for
the sake of others, ever has good dreams like these.

Again, in a dream or vision, you will be transformed
into a lord who forsakes palace, family and kin, as
well as the most exquisite pleasures the five senses
crave, to journey forth to the place of training at the
foot of a Bodhi tree where, seated on your Lion
Throne of Meditation, you will seek the Way until
seven days pass and you realize what 'the Wisdom
of the Buddhas' is.

Having thus succeeded to the Supreme Way, you will
arise and, turning the Wheel of the Dharma, proclaim
to the fourfold host of disciples My Teaching for
thousands of myriads of kalpas.

After giving voice to the undefiled Wondrous Dharma
and ferrying the countless sentient beings to the
Other Shore, you will then enter nirvana like a lamp
ceasing to smoke when its flame is extinguished.

If any of you in the evil ages to come give your voice to
this pre-eminent Dharma, you shall obtain a great
bounty such as the merits here foretold."

Precentor: Intone the following offertory

Precentor

From Great Compassion comes forth the Pure Dharma
Body, unborn, uncreated. We pray that the darkness
of our delusion may be illuminated by True Compassion. On this twenty-sixth day of January we come here
to celebrate the birth of the Highest Ancestor, Great
Master Dōgen. Entreating the Greatest Ancestor, Great
Master Keizan, to join us, we have devotedly prepared
incense, flowers, candles, sweet water, cakes, tea and
other delicacies as offerings; we have humbly gathered
the Sangha together to recite *The Scripture on the*

Conduct that Eases the Way. We offer the surpassing merits of our assembling here in recompense for their benevolence and kindness. We humbly pray that they will not abandon their compassionate hearts but take pity on those in the six realms of existence in all three worlds, that they will return in these last degenerate days of the Law to reveal the springtime of the Single Blossom with Its five leaves and that they will protect the disciples of later generations and assist our Ancestral Tradition for ages yet to come.

> **Community:**   Chant *The Three Homages.*
> **Assistant disciplinarian:**   Signal three bows.
> **Abbot and community:**   Make three bows, followed by three gratitude bows, and recess as usual.

READING OF *THE SCRIPTURE OF THE BUDDHA'S LAST TEACHINGS.*

Special note: In order to study the offering of Dharma for the Festival of the Buddha's Parinirvana, *The Scripture of the Buddha's Last Teachings* is recited after sunset on the first and ninth of the second month. The Scripture recited, the *Bussuihatsunehan Ryakusetsu Kyokaikyo,* can be translated as *The Scripture, The Teachings and Admonitions of Which Offer a Succinct Explanation of the Buddha's Parinirvana;* it can be either recited or chanted. When it is finished, the *Adoration of the Buddha's Relics* is chanted and there is one full bow after each chanting, making three chantings and three full bows. One must be very careful to chant the *Adoration of the Buddha's Relics* in an easy manner without holding in mind the idea that one is simply reciting a short litany. When reciting *The Scripture of the Buddha's Last Teachings*, the whole text is recited each day. When celebrating the Festival of the Buddha's Parinirvana on the fifteenth, one should recollect, with solemnity, the Buddha's Parinirvana especially whilst reciting *The Scripture of the Buddha's Last Teachings*. This recollection is done throughout the night in praise of the Buddha's virtue.

Sacristan: Hang picture of the Buddha's Parinirvana in ceremony hall, prepare incense, flowers and candles, ring bell in Dharma hall. (At Shasta Abbey this ceremony takes place in ceremony hall.)

Community: Process to Dharma hall.

Abbot or representative and chaplains: Abbot carries fountain sceptre. Process to Dharma hall.

Abbot: Go to altar, offer incense, return to bowing seat in usual way.

Assistant disciplinarian: Signal three bows.

Community and abbot: Make three full bows.

Community: Sit.

Precentor: Intone *The Scripture of the Buddha's Last Teachings*

Precentor

The Scripture of the Buddha's Last Teachings

Community: Chant *The Scripture of the Buddha's Last Teachings*

From the time when Shakyamuni first turned the Wheel of the Dharma to ferry Ajñata Kaundinya to the Other Shore until the last time He gave voice to the Dharma to carry Subhadra there, those responsive to being ferried had all been taken across and now He lay among the four twin sala trees about to enter parinirvana. At midnight when all was calm and not a sound was heard, He gave a summary explanation of the essentials of the Dharma to His disciples:

"O you monks, after I enter into eternal meditation, you should deeply honour, esteem and revere as precious the Ten Great and the Forty-eight Less Grave Precepts; just as darkness encounters brightness or a destitute person receives a treasure, so you should recognize these as your Great Teachers; whilst I abided in this world there were indeed none different from These for Me. Those of you who keep to these Pure Precepts are not to go about seeking to deal in commerce, barter or sale, or to live secure in field and home tending and nurturing family, clan, servants and animals; you should stay clear of any other kinds of profiteering and treasure hunting as if you were avoiding the fiery pit itself. Do not go about wantonly destroying or trampling down the vegetation, clearing the land and digging up the soil literally or figuratively. You should not mix and blend potions and nostrums, engage in forecasting fortune or misfortune, stare up at the positions of the stars and planets to infer how you should go forth based on their waxing and waning or make up calendars to try to compute and fix the future. When regulating the body, eat wholesome foods for self-sustenance. Do not go about participating in worldly affairs by circulating yourself as a messenger, do not engage in sorcery in search of some elixir of eternal life, seek to be intimate with people of influence and position or be close with those who treat others rudely or with contempt; none of these should you do. With an upright heart and appropriate thoughts you should seek to ferry others to the Other Shore. Do not go about trying to conceal your faults and shortcomings or display how different you are from deluded creatures. In making the four offerings which are your joy in awakening your heart, your reverence for the Dharma, your resolve to train and your practice, know your capacity and be content with that. Be quick to go about doing services and work but do not seek to amass tasks; these guides summarize the characteristics of keeping to the Precepts. The Precepts are what is appropriate to, and in accord with, the foundation and source of liberation, this is why they are called the Pratimokshas or what leads one toward liberation, accordingly, these Precepts can beget various meditations and the wisdom that eradicates suffering. O monks, keep to these Pure Precepts without giving others cause to slander you. If you can keep to these Pure Precepts you should know that this can have spiritual benefits for self and others; for those who do not have the Precepts, all goodness, merits and virtues cannot produce for them what they need to know. The Precepts are foremost for well-being, the abiding place of merit and virtue.

O you monks, since you can already abide in the Precepts, you should work on regulating your five senses; do not wantonly enter into the desires that arise from them. You are, for example, just as an ox-herder who holds his staff in hand and need but show it to his ox. Do not indulge in idleness, letting that which does not keep to the Precepts sow its seeds and grow its crops for, if you indulge your five senses, not only will your desires, which know no bounds, be ungovernable, they will also be as an unruly horse that, uncontrolled by a bridle, threatens to drag the trainer along until he tumbles into some hole. As if a kalpa's worth of injury and pain would come to an end in one lifetime! The calamities and misfortunes created by the thieving done by the five senses stretches from generation to generation; because their harm is exceedingly heavy, great caution is necessary. Wise is the one who is the governor and regulator of his senses and not their follower; treat them as though they were thieves; do not let them indulge in indolence and evasiveness. If you let them indulge themselves, they will soon enough see to their own obliteration for the Lord and master of these five senses is the discriminatory mind, therefore you should govern your mind well. The evasiveness of the discriminatory mind goes far beyond the dreadfulness of poisonous serpents, fierce beasts, ruthless robbers or blazing infernos, yet it is not enough merely to instruct it through metaphors for it is just like someone with a handful of honey who wheels about recklessly whilst focussing on the honey and fails to see the deep pit before him. It is like a crazed elephant without any restraints or like a monkey who has taken to the trees and prances about, leaping and jumping; only difficulties and suffering can constrain it; you should hasten to damp its ardour and not give it license to be indulgent for someone who indulges his mind loses his good practices. Govern it in a single situation and there will not be any affair you will be unable to manage; therefore, o monks, you should be diligent and skilfully progress by bending that discriminatory mind of yours to submission.

O you monks, when receiving food or drink you should look upon it as upon the ingesting of medicine; do not give rise to fluctuations in judgment by weighing it on the scales of good and bad. Be prompt to ingest it as a support for your body which removes hunger and thirst, at the same time be as the honeybee who, whilst gathering pollen from a flower, only takes the nectar and does not spoil or destroy the flower's colour, shape or scent. When receiving an offering from another, partake of it whilst ridding yourself of any feelings of irritation and dislike; to feel that you have not got very much, and therefore seek after more, destroys the good-hearted intention of the donor. It is just the same as with the shrewd person who measures the strength of an ox by how much it can bear and does not go to excess so that he wears out its strength.

O you monks, during the daytime practice the good Teachings with a diligent heart for there is no time to lose; the early evening and early morning should not be wasted. If you recite the Scriptures in the middle of the night, expend your breath by yourself; do not doze off and let your eyes close lest you allow your whole life to pass in vain without realization. Be mindful that the fires of impermanence incinerate all worlds so be quick in seeking to ferry yourself to the Other Shore and do not doze off, letting your eyes indeed close. The defiling passions rob, continuously waylay and slay people; they are far worse than a household filled with resentful people. How can you afford to doze off? You must arouse yourself and waken from your slumber; a defiling passion is a poisonous serpent asleep in your heart; it is like having a black viper in your room whilst you sleep. You must quickly snare this serpent by keeping to the Precepts, drive it off and remove it from your room; once the somnolent serpent has departed, you can sleep peacefully and in safety. If it does not depart and you close your eyes to it, you are the same as a person who lacks true modesty, that is you will lack awareness of your susceptibilities and remorse for your shortcomings, for, of all things splendrous, modesty is foremost; it is as a cast-iron restraint which can restrain others without recourse to any other thing. O monks, you should always act with a modest heart without neglecting it even for a short while; if you separate yourself from your feelings of modesty then you lose merit and virtue. When there are people who are modest then there will be good Teaching; if people lack modesty, there is no difference between them and birds or beasts.

O you monks, if someone should come to dismember your every joint, you should pacify your heart, not glare angrily or hatefully at the person, guard your mouth and refrain from spouting hot words of hate. If you indulge in a raging or resentful heart then you make yourself an obstacle in your own path and lose the benefits of your merit and virtue; forbear for virtue's sake and keep to the Precepts for, if you act in this way, you reach what seems impossible. The one who can behave with forbearance is called a great and powerful person. If there are those who cannot be joyful and delight in others, forbearance will accept the poison of their malice and curses as a person drinking the Sweet Dew. He or she who, namelessly entering the Way, is indeed the one with discriminate wisdom. Why is this? Because the mischief from anger, hatred and resentment can break one's own Teachings and destroy another's reputation so that now, and in the future, people will not be delighted to meet them or you. You should realize that an angry heart depends on a fierce flame, so be on guard, without crossing over into anger and resentment, lest you let these thieves of kalpas of merit and virtue gain entrance. When common folk embrace their greeds they are people who walk not in the Way; they lack the Teaching to restrain themselves so that their anger can still harbour resentment and find fault with others. When monks walk in the Way they are people who do not hanker after things so that attachments, which give rise to anger and resentment, become all but impossible. Just as one who, at the first sound of thunder amidst the chill and bracing clouds, starts up a fire, it is not fitting to enkindle anger at the first signs of coldness or trouble.

O you monks, you should polish your heads and, having relinquished ornaments and other adornments, wear appropriate robes of a subdued colour; holding a suitable vessel in your hands, beg alms for your livelihood. Look at yourself in the following way. If arrogance or pride arise you should quickly eradicate them; arrogance and pride are not seemly even for common folk who follow worldly ways so how much less are they seemly for a person who has left home to enter the Way. Will you yield yourself to those attitudes when you go forth to beg alms for the sake of liberation?

O you monks, the mind that is flattering and fawning acts contrary to the Way, therefore keep your heart honest and forthright for you should realize that flattery and fawning are merely done for the sake of imposing on others or making fools of them. O monks, maintain an upright heart which will serve you as the foundation for your honesty and forthrightness.

O you monks, recognise the person who has many cravings; his misery and troubles are many because he seeks for many benefits, gains and advantages. The person of few cravings is free from seeking after things or yearning for them, hence he is free of such sufferings; he desires little, only esteeming what is fitting for his spiritual training and practice; by desiring little, so much more is he able to bring forth fine merits and virtues. The person of few desires is free of flattery and fawning when searching out the intentions of others. The heart of someone who behaves with few desires is, as a consequence, composed and free from gloom, anxiety, sorrow or fear; when coming in contact with things, he finds a surplus for there is never an insufficiency. The one who has few desires has Nirvana for this is the name for 'having few desires'.

O you monks, if you wish to be free from miseries and woes, look into contentment which is synonymous with knowing what is enough; the Teaching of contentment is none other than the location of true wealth, ease, security and peace. The person who is contented, though he sleeps upon the bare ground, is still at ease and satisfied; someone who is discontented, even if he were ensconced in a celestial palace, would still not find this tallying with his ideas and tastes. The one who is discontented, though rich, is poor; the person who is contented, though poor, is rich. The one who is discontented always does what his five desires latch onto; he does that which causes grief to, and arouses the compassionate pity of, one who is contented. This is what I mean by the term 'contentment'.

O you monks, if you seek to be tranquil and quiet, liberated from the insistence of the defiling passions, at ease and content, then you should part company with confusion and bustle and dwell at your ease in some solitary place. The person who dwells in quietude continually forsakes what those in the heavens esteem so highly amongst themselves, therefore withdraw from those about you, as well as from other crowds, and, in a place of solitude apart from them, reflect on the source of the eradication of suffering at your leisure. If you are one who enjoys the company of others then you will take on the woes of their company, just as with a flock of birds that gather in some huge tree, there is the lament of dead branches breaking off under their weight. When the world binds itself around us, we drown in the suffering of such company just as an old elephant, sunk down in the mire, is unable to drag himself out.

O you monks, if you are diligent in your devotion to progress, training will not be difficult for you, therefore be diligent and devote yourselves to progress just as a small stream, ever flowing, can bore holes in rocks. If the mind of the trainee is often inattentive and remiss, it will be just the same as making a fire by friction and blowing on it before it is hot enough to catch ablaze; although your desire to train can blaze up, the fires of training are hard to arrive at. This is what I call 'devotion to progress'.

O you monks, seek fine understanding, search out good assistance and do not neglect being mindful. If you are one who does not neglect mindfulness, the thieves of passional defilement will not be able to enter, therefore, you monks, always keep your minds alert, for the one who loses mindfulness loses his merits and virtues. When the strength of your mindfulness is constant and vigorous, though the five desires would break in to rob you, they will do you no harm; you will be as one who puts on armour before entering a battle and will have nothing to fear. This is what I call 'not neglecting mindfulness'.

O you monks, when your mind is kept alert, then you are in meditation; because your mind is in meditation, you are able to know the world, birth and death, as well as the characteristics of all things, therefore you monks should always study and practice the ways of meditation with finest diligence. When you achieve meditation, your heart is not in turmoil or your mind scattered; just as a household that would be frugal with water arranges dikes and pond banks carefully, so a trainee does likewise. Therefore, for the sake of the water of discriminate wisdom, practice meditation well that you may prevent the loss of that water through leaks caused by the defiling passions. This is what I call 'doing meditation'.

O you monks, when you have discriminate wisdom, you will not be attached to desires; by constant self-reflection and watching what you do, you will not bring about any loss through the defiling passions; within My Teachings this is what can bring you to liberation. If someone denies this, not only is he not a person of the Way, he is also not an ordinary, everyday person either; indeed, there is no name for such a one. Genuine discriminate wisdom is the sturdy craft that ferries others across the sea of old age, disease and death; it is also a great bright lamp for the darkness of ignorance, a wonderful curative for all disease and suffering. It is a sharp axe for felling the trees of defiling passions, therefore you monks should improve yourselves by means of this wisdom which you attain through hearing, thinking about and putting into practice My Teachings. When someone has the radiance of this wisdom then, though he be blind, he will clearly see what people are. This is what 'discriminating wisdom' is.

O you monks, if your mind plays around with all kinds of theories and opinions it will be confused and in disorder and, though you have left home to be a monk, you have still not yet realized liberation; therefore, o monks, quickly abandon your disordered mind and your playing around with your theories and notions. If you wish to enjoy the pleasure that comes from calmness and the extinction of defiling passions, thoroughly eliminate the affliction of playing around in your head. This is what I mean by 'not playing around with theories and opinions'.

O you monks, you should wholeheartedly discard all forms of looseness and self-indulgence in favour of merits and virtues just as you would keep away from a malicious thief. What the World-honoured One desires with His great compassion is to benefit all by means of their ultimate realization of their identity with Buddha. Be it deep in the mountains, in an uninhabited valley or under some tree, your place of seclusion is your abode of peace. Keep in mind what you have received of the Teachings; do not let yourself be forgetful of Them and thereby lose Them; always be as diligent as possible in your practice and mastery of Them; the unreality of the unconditioned after death spawns gloom and regret. Like a good physician, I understand illness and prescribe curatives for you to take; not to take them is not the doctor's fault. I also resemble a skilled guide who leads others to a clear pathway; not to heed him and not to travel the path is not the mistake of the guide. If you, in your sufferings, have any doubts about the Four Noble Truths, you can forthwith ask Me about them for, to fail to eradicate your doubts, is indeed to fail to seek for certainty."

The World-honoured One then made this same offer twice again but, among those present, none asked. Why was this? Because, within the assembly, none had any doubts.

Then Aniruddha, the Buddha's chief disciple with divine vision, scrutinizing the minds of the assembled, said to the Buddha, "O World-honoured One, the moon can make us hot and the sun can be cold to us. The Buddha has told us that the Four Noble Truths should not make us different from each other. The Buddha has also told us that the reality of the Truth of suffering is that suffering, which is the inability to make ourselves happy, exists, that the reality of the defiling passions is the cause of that suffering and this cause is not different for any of us, that if suffering is extinguished then this cause is extinguished because, when a cause is eliminated, its fruits are also eliminated and that the path to eliminating it is, in reality, the Path of Truth and there is no other way. O World-honoured One, these monks have certainty and are free of doubts about the Four Noble Truths. If there is anyone within this assembly who has not yet accomplished what needs to be done then, upon seeing the Buddha enter parinirvana, let him give rise to feelings of pity for others. If you have already penetrated His Teachings you have heard what the Buddha has voiced which is to help ferry all to the Other Shore; it is as a flash of lightning seen in the night which helps one see the Way. If what needs to be done is already accomplished and you have already crossed the sea of suffering, keep just this thought in mind, the parinirvana of the World-honoured One is exactly the same as shouldering the burden of all ills!"

Although Aniruddha spoke these words, the assembly had all thoroughly penetrated the meaning of the Four Noble Truths. The World-honoured One, desiring to help all in this great assembly to realize certainty, spoke to them from His heart of great compassion,

"O you monks, do not harbour grief and woe within your bosoms. Were I to abide in this world for the space of a whole kalpa I must still enter into eternal meditation; to remain for such a length of time, and not ultimately to depart, is an impossibility. The Teaching that to spiritually benefit yourself by training benefits others contains all; were I to abide longer there would still be no more to obtain from Me than this. As for those who should be able to ferry others to the Other Shore, if humans are in some heaven they have already been completely carried across; those not yet carried across have also all already created the cause for their being ferried; you yourselves are now already past this. O My disciples, the Principles which I have extended, expanded and employed are the Dharma-body of the Tathagata which always abides and is not extinguished, therefore you should realize that the world is not forever, of necessity we part from it, so do not cling to grief for the world is ever thus. Be diligent in your devotion to progress and quickly seek liberation; with the clarity of your discriminate wisdom and insight eradicate the darkness of delusion for the world is truly susceptible to fear and mistrust and wants strength and stability. Since I now enter into eternal meditation, you should strive to rid yourself of what I call 'the embodied self' as though it were something foul that was polluting you, for it is this illusory self which will sink down into the great ocean of birth, old age, disease and death. To get rid of it is like recovering from a bad illness. How can any of you, who has the wit to try, fail to feel anything but joy when you have freed yourself from the false ego for then you will have slain the malicious thief that it is?

O you monks, with wholehearted devotion always seek to get back on the path. All that is mutable or immutable in all worlds defeats and destroys the signs of uncertainty. Bring them to a halt! Do not ask Me to say more for the time is nigh when I would pass and I wish for my parinirvana. These are My last Teachings and instructions."

Assistant disciplinarian: Do one ring-down for community to spread mats.
Community: Spread mats fully and stand on them.
Precentor: Intone *Adoration of the Buddha's Relics* after community has spread mats

Precentor

*A*doration of the Buddha's Relics

Community: Chant the *Adoration of the Buddha's Relics* (to be found on page 43)

165

three times, make one full bow after each repetition.

Precentor: Recite the customary offertory for Shakyamuni Buddha (to be found on page 96).

Community: Chant *The Three Homages*.

Assistant disciplinarian: Signal three bows.

Community: Make three bows, followed by three gratitude bows.

Abbot: Recess.

Community: Recess.

Special note: Usual late afternoon ceremony is omitted. Chanting and bowing to the Scripture of the *Adoration of the Buddha's Relics* is the basic ceremony. It is for this reason that the comments about the chanting of the *Adoration of the Buddha's Relics* were made in the special note at the beginning of this ceremony.

MINDFUL RECITATION AT THE SHRINE OF THE GUARDIAN DEITY.

Sacristan: This takes place after sunset. Prepare flowers and candles at the Shrine of the Guardian Deity; if weather too inclement place table in eastern section of ceremony hall (south door of ceremony hall in Shasta Abbey) and cover it with that which is similar to the altar of the Guardian Deity.

Assistant disciplinarian: Hit time blocks whilst inspecting incense arrangements in all halls.

Sacristy acolyte: Ring large bell as is usual for a Mindful Recitation for the Ten Buddhas.

Community: Process to Guardian Deity's Shrine or hall, line up on either side as would be usual for a Mindful Recitation for the Ten Buddhas.

Abbot or representative: Process to hall, circumambulate it, offer incense at all altars, arrive at Guardian Deity's Shrine or altar last.

Chaplains: Follow abbot carrying incense sticks for each altar and incense box.

Assistant disciplinarian: When abbot approaches Guardian Deity's Shrine or altar, strike small gong seven times.

Abbot: Arrive at Guardian Deity's Shrine or altar.

Special note: At abbot's discretion, bows are made with full mat, Z-folded mat or standing.

Assistant disciplinarian: Lead bows as indicated by abbot, making usual ring-down on signal gong if appropriate.

Community and abbot: Make three bows as indicated by abbot.

Abbot: Bow to monks on both sides, take one or two steps towards altar table, make deep monjin, go to altar table, offer incense, Great Monk's Offertory, return to place, sit on chair.

Sacristy acolyte: Strike cymbals for three ring-downs.

Precentor: Leave place, go to altar, inspect fire in censer, stand on left side of altar (right when facing it) with back to Guardian Deity.

Sacristy acolyte: Do second three ring-downs with cymbals.

Precentor: Go to abbot, escort him to altar.

Sacristy acolyte: Strike cymbals five times as abbot is escorted to altar and returns.

Abbot: Go to altar led by precentor, offer incense, return to place.

Precentor: Lead first right side and then left side of community to altar to offer incense.

Community: Follow precentor, offer incense in gratitude, make monjin.

Precentor: Go to altar, hold Mindful Recitation text, cense it in smoke from incense burner, return to place, recite following Mindful Recitation

◢ **Precentor** ◣

The spring breezes fan over the fields and the emperor of greening rules everywhere; winter's three months' governance has come to an end; the sun, following its proper course, marks the return of spring; three months have passed without disaster and the whole community is at ease. We recite the names of the Great Buddhas of Myriad Virtues as we humbly report to you, the Guardian Deity of all the monastery halls; out of respect, we take refuge in the Holy Sangha as we pray aloud.

> **Community:** Chant *The Names of the Ten Buddhas,* to be found on page 104.
> **Sacristy acolyte:** Ring bell at the chanting of each name as is usual for the Mindful Recitation for the Closing of the Meditation Hall.
> **Precentor:** Recite the following offertory

◢ **Precentor** ◣

Assembled here, we offer all the merits of this recitation to the nagas and deities of this place who guard and protect the True Law. Bowing, we pray that your divine light will assist us, that you will open wide your meritorious deeds, that this temple and its sacred Precepts will prosper and that you will grant us impartial joy unending.

> **Community:** Chant *The Three Homages.*
> **Assistant disciplinarian:** Signal three bows.
> **Community:** Make three bows as indicated by abbot, followed by three gratitude bows.
> **Abbot:** Recess.

Community: Recess.

Special note: This offertory is used at Mindful Recitation for the Guardian Deity ceremonies throughout the year following.

READING OF *THE SCRIPTURE OF THE BUDDHA'S LAST TEACHINGS.*

Special note: At Shasta Abbey this ceremony takes place in ceremony hall.

Sacristy acolyte: When Mindful Recitation of *The Names of the Ten Buddhas* is finished, ring Dharma hall bell one full ring-down.

Head novice: Lead community from Guardian Deity's Shrine to Dharma hall, take usual places.

Abbot: Carry fountain sceptre, process to hall, go to altar, offer incense and sweet water, return to bowing seat.

Assistant disciplinarian: Signal three bows.

Community and abbot: Make three full bows.

Special Note: From here this ceremony is identical with that for the Reading of *The Scripture of the Buddha's Last Teachings* on the first.

THE OPENING OF THE GUEST HOUSE.

Guest master: After noon meal, go round the dormitories reciting the *Invocation for the Removal of Disasters,* which is found on page 114.

Guest house first acolyte: Carry stick incense to each room for guest master to offer.

Guest house second acolyte: Carry Holy Water vessel and asperge to each room for guest master.

Guest master: Carry hand-held censer, offer incense at each room, asperge each room, open guest house doors, welcome all monks who wish to stay in the monastery whilst on angya, show them to their dormitories, take tea with them, make polite conversation.

THE SHUTTING DOWN OF THE FURNACES.

Maintenance monk: This day is considered the time to shut down furnaces and heating stoves. Furnaces and stoves in the meditation hall and dormitories are shut down and fires for heating rooms are not laid. Whilst going around the temple to each hall or room with a fire or furnace making certain that all is safe and closed down, carry a hand-held censer, offer incense in each place, recite the *Invocation for the Removal of Disasters,* which is found on page 114.

Maintenance acolyte: Carry incense sticks, for each hall or room, for maintenance monk.

Community: No longer wear mōses to ceremonies or other functions, fold hands without covering them with sleeves.

THE CLOSING OF THE GUEST HOUSE.

Guest master: After breakfast shut down the guest house dormitories and discontinue allowing visiting monks on angya to stay, go round the dormitories reciting the *Invocation for the Removal of Disasters,* which is found on page 114.

Guest house first acolyte: Carry stick incense to each room for guest master to offer.

Guest house second acolyte: Carry Holy Water vessel and asperge to each room for guest master.

Guest master: Carry hand-held censer, offer incense at each room, asperge each room.

Special note: The Japanese term for this is shikata. Because no more visiting monks can be permitted to come and stay since the number of available places is filled even though it is in the middle of the period between monastic retreats, signs reading "Visits from Monks on Angya Discontinued" are hung in front of community dormitories.

MINDFUL RECITATION AT THE SHRINE OF THE GUARDIAN DEITY.

Special note: This takes place after sunset. This ceremony is the same as that at the end of winter on the fourteenth day of the second month. The following Mindful Recitation is made by the precentor

Precentor

Balmy breezes fan over the fields and the emperor of heat rules everywhere. This is a time when, in obedience to the Lord of the Law, we take not a step from the temple; these are the days for protecting the lives of the Buddha's disciples. We have assembled the whole community in all humility and respectfully visit your sacred shrine; we recite the names of the Great Buddhas of Myriad Virtues and offer the merit therefrom to you, the Guardian Deity of all the monastic halls. We pray for your divine protection that we may be able to accomplish this retreat; out of respect we take refuge in the Holy Sangha as we pray aloud.

Community: Recite *The Names of the Ten Buddhas* (to be found on page 104) as in other Mindful Recitations at the Shrine of the Guardian Deity.

175

THE OFFERING OF TEA BY THE
SENIOR OFFICERS OF THE TEMPLE.

Head novice's assistant: After noon meal, go to room of head novice and assist in preparations, wait.

Head novice: Put on Kesa, set up incense stand in own room, keep incense lit, await arrival of seniormost officer.

Seniormost officer's acolyte: Prepare offering stand draped with square cloth in room of seniormost officer.

Seniormost officer: After noon meal, put on Kesa, place "Sweet Water" sign on offering stand, hold stand aloft and process to room of head novice.

Seniormost officer: Enter room of head novice, cense sign in incense smoke, place it next to incense stand, recite following invitation

Seniormost officer

This evening the senior officers are conducting a special tea in the meditation hall. It is respectfully hoped that you will attend out of your kind generosity and compassion.

Seniormost officer: Make one bow to head novice without spreading mat, return to own room.

Head novice: Return bow, escort seniormost officer out, request assistant to hang sign on board outside meditation hall.

Head novice's assistant: Hang sign.

Chaplain: Prepare an incense stand in the abbot's or representative's quarters.

Abbot or representative: Put on Kesa, await arrival of seniormost officer.

Seniormost officer: Put on Kesa, process to abbot's or representative's quarters, offer incense, spread mat, recite following invitation

Seniormost officer

Tonight we are giving a tea in the meditation hall especially for the head novice and the whole community. Out of respect, we hope that you, O Great Priest, out of your kind generosity and compassion will, in particular, deign to attend.

Seniormost officer: Return to dormitory, request acolyte to hang "Brewing Sweet Water" sign in meditation hall.

Seniormost officer's acolyte: Hang up sign.

Tea monk: Around 4:00 P.M., before the Mindful Recitation at the Shrine of the Guardian Deity ceremony has started, request acolyte to set up special seat for the chief guest in the meditation hall (on tan nearest precentor's stand on northwest side of hall; arrange for monk who usually sits there to take another seat during ceremony).

Tea monk's acolyte: Set up seat. After the offertory of the Mindful Recitation at the Shrine of the Guardian Deity is complete, strike tea drum one full cycle. At Shasta Abbey, great bell is used in place of tea drum and rung one ring-down.

Assistant disciplinarian: Ring meditation hall bell in usual manner.

Head novice: As bell rings, lead community from Guardian Deity's Shrine to meditation hall.

Community: Follow head novice, stand in front of own places in meditation hall.

Senior officers: Process to own seats in meditation hall.

Abbot: Wait at Guardian Deity's Shrine until meditation hall bell has ceased, process to meditation hall, take seat.

Seniormost officer: When all are in their places, go stand before head novice, invite head novice to be seated in the chief guest's seat, go to clerical officer (Shoki), make monjin, return to head novice, lead head novice to chief guest's seat.

Head novice: Follow seniormost officer to chief guest's seat, be seated.

Community: Make monjin in gratitude to senior officers for their offering of tea, be seated.

Senior officers: Be seated.

Tea monk's first acolyte: Serve tea first to head novice, then to abbot.

Tea monk's acolytes: Serve tea in usual way to community and to senior officers.

Community: Take tea in usual way.

Tea monk's acolytes: When tea is finished, collect cups in usual way.

Seniormost officer: Rise, lead senior officers to stand in front of abbot.

Senior officers: Rise, follow seniormost officer, stand in line before abbot.

Abbot: Rise, make gesture as if spreading mat, recite following

Abbot

The simple Sweet Water offered today is especially bathed by the benevolence and compassion that have descended repeatedly into it. The humble expression of our emotions does not equal the depth of our feelings.

Abbot: Make gesture as if spreading mat a second time, recite following

Abbot

As the days gradually become warmer we respectfully pray that the health and happiness in the daily life of the chief priest of the temple meet with ten thousand blessings.

Abbot: Spread mat, make three bows to senior officers and community.
Senior officers and community: Receive abbot's bows with gasshō. Senior officers return to seats.
Community: Rise.
Assistant disciplinarian: Signal three bows.
Senior officers and community: Spread mats in Z-fold, make three bows to abbot.
Abbot: Receive bows in gasshō, spread mat, make one bow.
All: Pick up mats.
Community: Process to gaitan door of meditation hall, each side of hall lining up on its respective side of door.

Abbot: Make monjin, process from hall, return to quarters.

Community: Make monjin as abbot leaves.

Monks of western hall (north side at Shasta Abbey):   Make monjin to senior officers, process from hall, return to dormitories.

Head Novice: Face senior officers, spread mat in Z-fold, make one bow, pick up mat, process from hall, return to room.

Senior officers: Make monjin in return for bow.

Seniormost officer: Offer incense at main altar to thank Sangha for Their company, make monjin.

Assistant disciplinarian: Ring down meditation hall bell once.

Monks of eastern hall (south side at Shasta Abbey):   Make monjin to senior officers, process from hall, return to dormitories.

Assistant disciplinarian: Ring down drum three times.

Senior officers: Process from hall, return to dormitories.

CIRCUMAMBULATION
OF THE DORMITORIES.

Chaplain: Put up sign saying "Circumambulation of the Dormitories" before breakfast outside meditation hall.

Sacristan: After breakfast, place seat for abbot in each house, dormitory and office along with incense, flowers, tea or sweet water. At Shasta Abbey each monk and department will set up room.

Community: Put things in room, dormitory or office in order, wait outside each room, dormitory or office for abbot's circumambulation since abbot will be inspecting the rooms, dormitories and offices.

Chaplains: After breakfast, listen to the abbot's wishes.

Fifth chaplain: Make a triple ring-down on time block in front of abbot's quarters.

Abbot or representative: Upon hearing ring-down, leave quarters.

Chaplains and acolytes: Follow abbot.

Guest-handling chaplain: Carry incense burner and incense box.

Senior officers' acolyte: Strike time block in front of senior officers' dormitory three times.

Senior officers and monks working with them in their offices: Gather and line up at the entry of room, dormitory or office to welcome abbot.

Abbot: Enter room, dormitory or office, take seat.

> **Governing officers and assembled monks:** Follow abbot into room where abbot is seated.
>
> **Senior officers:** Present abbot with tea or sweet water.
>
> **Abbot:** Inquire into any irregularity noticed on way to seat, listen to state of affairs reported by senior officers concerning state of rooms, dormitories or offices, rise, leave seat.
>
> **Senior officers:** When abbot stands up, step towards abbot.
>
> **All monks assembled:** Rise, spread mats, recite the following

Bowing, we receive this visit from your priestly Dharma entourage. The humble expression of our emotions does not equal the depth of our feelings.

> **All monks present:** Make first full bow, recite the following

As the days gradually warm up we respectfully pray that the health and happiness in the daily life of the Chief Priest of the temple meet with ten thousand blessings.

> **All monks present:** Make second and third full bows, pick up mats, place folded mats on floor, make another three full bows.
>
> **Abbot:** Place folded mat on floor, make one bow.
>
> **Senior officers and assembled monks:** Go outside room, dormitory or office to see abbot's departure and follow abbot immediately to the next room, dormitory or office.

Special note: Each room, dormitory or office is visited in the same way, the same words are spoken and the same bows made. It is usual to make the rounds from the eastern corridor and, through the main gate, to the western corridor, in accordance with the most convenient route, to give the abbot access to all dormitories, rooms and offices. When there is no senior officer present, the head of the particular room, dormitory or office that the abbot is visiting proffers the tea or sweet water after the abbot has sat down. If the abbot does not enter the room, dormitory or office and sit down, the ceremony is not performed although abbot will inspect each room, dormitory or office with the occupant or occupants standing respectfully outside the door whilst abbot does so. After abbot's inspection, all follow the abbot. When the rounds of the rooms, dormitories and offices are finished, the whole community will be following the abbot. When the Dharma hall is reached, the following takes place:

Abbot: Clasp hands, face south, stand before steps to Dharma seat. (At Shasta Abbey this is done in ceremony hall; abbot stands in front of altar facing meditation hall, monks face altar.)

Community: Face north (altar), make deep monjin.

Abbot: Make monjin, return to quarters.

Community: Return to dormitories.

HEAD NOVICE'S PRESENTATION OF
A FUNDAMENTAL DOCTRINE AND TEA.

Special note: The abbot's incense chaplain receives the abbot's or representative's instructions and prepares the chapter that the abbot wishes the head novice to present. This is usually a topic from the *Shōyōroku* but some other Scripture or topic is fine.

Sacristan: Ring evening bell.

Tea master's acolyte: Prepare for the serving of tea in tea hall or ceremony hall.

Sacristan: Provide seat in front of hall for abbot; when this ceremony is done during monks' retreat, provide places on both sides for all those from western and back halls; put incense stand in centre of hall with incense box on it as is done for abbatical tea ceremony.

Tea master's acolyte: When bell ringing has stopped, strike tea drum in usual way. (At Shasta Abbey great bell is rung in usual way if no tea drum.)

Community: Wear Kesas; when hearing tea drum, gather in tea hall, take places for serving of tea.

Abbot: Enter tea hall.

Incense chaplain: Follow abbot, carry offering stand on which copy of doctrine text lies.

Abbot and community: Bow, take seats.

Incense chaplain: Place text on stand on abbot's left.

Abbot: Inform the community thus

Abbot

Tomorrow I shall turn over the Dharma Seat to Rev. ..., the head novice, and have him/her give a talk on ... text.

Incense chaplain: Rise, hold offering stand in both hands with scriptural text on it, place stand in front of head novice, return to seat.

Head novice: Rise, hold scriptural text aloft, go to incense stand, cense scriptural text in smoke from incense, place scriptural text before stand, step back, spread mat, make three full bows (these are called the "Bows of Acceptance").

Abbot: At last bow, bow once in response.

Head novice: When bows are finished, pick up mat, hold scriptural text aloft, go in front of abbot, ask abbot to lecture by making monjin, return to place.

Abbot: Accept right to lecture from head novice, open Scripture presented by head novice, make lecture up to gatha section.

Special note: There are occasions when the lecture on such a doctrine is done by someone from the western hall other than the abbot.

Incense chaplain: When lecture is finished, offer tea to abbot in usual way.

Tea master's acolytes: Serve community with tea in usual way.

Special note: After second serving, tea cups are collected in usual way by tea master's acolytes.

Tea master's acolyte: Ring down drum three times.

Assistant disciplinarian: Strike signal gong twice.

Community: Rise.

Abbot and community: Bow together.

Abbot: Recess from hall.

Community: Recess from hall.

GREAT FESTIVAL OF
THE RENEWAL OF VOWS.

Special note: This is identical to the Abridged Form of the Renewal of Vows (see page 117) except that *The Scripture of Brahma's Net* is always recited in full and there is no tea.

OPENING OF BATHS FOR SUMMER.

(Sweat Baths)

Special note: In addition to the opening of the baths on four and nine days during the three months from the beginning of the seventh to the end of the ninth month, there are also 'sweat baths' on the second and seventh days. 'Sweat baths' use hot water to induce sweating but, in actuality, are the same as taking a bath in hot water. After the mid-day meal a sign reading 'Sweat Baths' is hung on the bath house. The bathing of the Holy One, the circumambulation of the corridors and the striking of the time blocks and bath drum are not done; in place of the drum, clappers are struck, all else is the same as on any bath day.

MINDFUL RECITATION AT THE SHRINE OF THE GUARDIAN DEITY.

Special note: This takes place after sunset. The order of ceremony is the same as on the fourteenth day of the second month. The following Mindful Recitation text is used

Precentor

Golden breezes fan over the fields and the emperor of frost rules everywhere. The time is as that when the Buddha, Lord of Enlightenment, commenced the monks' retreat; it is the day of our being a whole year older in the Dharma. Three months have passed without disaster and the whole Community is at ease. We recite the names of the Great Buddhas of Myriad Virtues as we humbly report to you, the Guardian Deity of all the monastery halls; out of respect, we take refuge in the Holy Sangha as we pray aloud.

Community: Recite *The Names of the Ten Buddhas* (to be found on page 104) as in other Mindful Recitations at the Shrine of the Guardian Deity.

189

MEMORIAL FOR THE TWO ANCESTORS DŌGEN AND KEIZAN.

Special note: This ceremony is identical to the Memorial for the Two Ancestors Dōgen and Keizan celebrated on the twenty-eighth day of each month except that *The Scripture on the Immeasurable Life of the Tathagata* (to be found on page 131) is used and the following offertory is recited

Precentor

From Great Compassion comes forth the Pure Dharma Body, unborn, uncreated. We pray that the darkness of our delusion may be illuminated by True Compassion. On this twenty-ninth day of September, we are gathered here to offer incense, flowers, candles, cakes and tea in commemoration of the deaths of the Highest Ancestor, Great Master Dōgen, and the Greatest Ancestor, Great Master Keizan. Out of gratitude we wish to offer them the merits of this recitation of *The Scripture on the Immeasurable Life of the Tathagata.* We humbly pray that they will not abandon their compassionate hearts but will take pity on those in the six realms of existence in all three worlds, that they will return in these last degenerate days of the Law to reveal the springtime of the Single Blossom with Its five leaves and that they will protect the disciples of later generations and assist our Ancestral tradition for ages yet to come.

THE TURNING ON OF THE FURNACES.

Maintenance monk: Go round temple turning on furnaces and heaters, carry hand-held censer, offer incense and recite the *Invocation for the Removal of Disasters* (to be found on page 114) in each hall or wherever there is an open fireplace.

Maintenance acolyte: Carry incense stick for maintenance monk to offer in each hall or room where there is an open fireplace.

Community: From this day on, mōses may be worn and sleeves may cover folded hands.

MINDFUL RECITATION AT THE SHRINE OF THE GUARDIAN DEITY.

Special note: This takes place after sunset. The ceremonial procedures are the same as those on the fourteenth day of the second month. The Mindful Recitation is as follows

Precentor

The northerly winds fan across the fields, the emperor of darkness rules everywhere. As we take especial care to prepare for the ceremony of the three-month winter retreat we have established plans to shelter ourselves from the hundred days of cold and have assembled the community here to reverently pay your sacred shrine a visit; we recite the names of the Great Buddhas of Myriad Virtues and offer the merit therefrom to you, the Guardian Deity of all the monastic halls. We pray for your divine protection that we may be able to accomplish this retreat and, out of respect, we take refuge in the Holy Sangha as we pray aloud.

Community: Recite *The Names of the Ten Buddhas* (to be found on page 104) as in other Mindful Recitations at the Shrine of the Guardian Deity.

THE OFFERING OF TEA BY THE SENIOR OFFICERS OF THE TEMPLE.

Special note: This follows upon the Mindful Recitation at the Shrine of the Guardian Deity and is performed in the meditation hall. The ceremonial procedures are the same as those on the fourteenth day of the fifth month. The abbot or representative, upon spreading his mat the second time, chants, "As the days gradually grow colder..." rather than the words that are used on the fourteenth day of the fifth month.

THE FESTIVAL OF THE BIRTH OF THE GREATEST ANCESTOR KEIZAN.

Special note: This is identical with the ceremony for the birth of Eihei Dōgen except the name is changed in the offertory (see page 140).

MEMORIAL FOR THE SECOND CHINESE ANCESTOR TAISŌ EKA.

Special note: This ceremony is identical with that held on the twenty-ninth day of any month for the Two Ancestors except that *The Shurangama Litany* is used (to be found on page 56) and the title and name of Taisō Eka are substituted in the offertory.

SWEEPING OUT THE SOOT FROM VARIOUS HALLS.

Special note: This is done after breakfast. A chaplain plans out work in advance with chief cook, extern sacristan (Shisui) and maintenance monk.

Chaplain: After breakfast notify those in meditation hall and various dormitories, strike the work drum.

Community: Omit normal cleaning, receive instructions from superiors and clean whole monastery. Areas in and around stoves in kitchen should be swept clean of soot by male members of community.

Special note: All day is a community work day which is exempt from all ceremonial observances. In order to have fine weather, one need not be limited to thirteenth day of this month to do this task.

Maintenance monk: Go to each large furnace and open fireplace.

Maintenance acolyte: Carry asperge bowl and incense sticks. There should be enough sticks for one for each place where there is a furnace or open fireplace.

Maintenance monk: Carry hand-held censer, recite, together with acolytes, the *Invocation for the Removal of Disasters* (to be found on page 114) at each furnace or open fireplace, offer incense stick, powdered incense, and asperge the furnace or fireplace.

MINDFUL RECITATION AT THE SHRINE OF THE GUARDIAN DEITY.

Special note: This takes place after sunset. The ceremonial procedures are the same as those for the fourteenth day of the second month. The precentor recites the following Mindful Recitation

Precentor

Transforming work progresses on unseen, passing time circles round again. Wholeheartedly do we pray for peace and tranquillity during the four approaching seasons as we endeavour to open up to the joy of the Threefold Source. We have assembled the community here to reverently pay your sacred shrine a visit; we recite the names of the Great Buddhas of Myriad Virtues and offer the merit therefrom to you and the other Guardian Deities of all the monastic halls. Out of respect, we take refuge in the Holy Sangha as we pray aloud.

Community: Recite *The Names of the Ten Buddhas* (to be found on page 104) as in other Mindful Recitations at the Shrine of the Guardian Deity.

NOTES.

NOTES.

NOTES.

NOTES.